Champions of Access to Knowledge

 OPEN TEXT

All digital forms of access to our high-quality open texts are entirely FREE! All content is reviewed for excellence and is wholly adaptable; custom editions are produced by Lyryx for those adopting Lyryx assessment. Access to the original source files is also open to anyone!

 ONLINE ASSESSMENT

We have been developing superior online formative assessment for more than 15 years. Our questions are continuously adapted with the content and reviewed for quality and sound pedagogy. To enhance learning, students receive immediate personalized feedback. Student grade reports and performance statistics are also provided.

 SUPPORT

Access to our in-house support team is available 7 days/week to provide prompt resolution to both student and instructor inquiries. In addition, we work one-on-one with instructors to provide a comprehensive system, customized for their course. This can include adapting the text, managing multiple sections, and more!

 INSTRUCTOR SUPPLEMENTS

Additional instructor resources are also freely accessible. Product dependent, these supplements include: full sets of adaptable slides and lecture notes, solutions manuals, and multiple choice question banks with an exam building tool.

Contact Lyryx Today!
info@lyryx.com

Intermediate Financial Accounting

by Glenn Arnold & Suzanne Kyle

Edited by Athabasca University

Version 2017 — Revision C

BE A CHAMPION OF OER!

Contribute suggestions for improvements, new content, or errata:

A new topic

A new example

An interesting new question

Any other suggestions to improve the material

Contact Lyryx at info@lyryx.com with your ideas.

Lyryx Learning Team

Bruce Bauslaugh

Peter Chow

Nathan Friess

Stephanie Keyowski

Claude Laflamme

Martha Laflamme

Jennifer MacKenzie

Tamsyn Murnaghan

Bogdan Sava

Ryan Yee

LICENSE

Table of Contents

Chapter 12 Solutions

EXERCISE 12–1

a. CL

b. CL

c. CL

d. CL

e. Both

f. Not recorded

g. CL and possibly NCL if goods/services provided more than one year in the future

h. NCL, unless decommissioning will happen within one year, then CL

i. Not recorded unless lawsuit is settled/resolved

j. CL

k. CL

l. Both

m. CL or NCL, depending on term of note

n. CL

o. Both, depending on expiry date of points

EXERCISE 12–2

a.

General Journal				
Date	Account/Explanation	PR	Debit	Credit
	Accounts payable		8,000	
	Note payable			8,000

b.

General Journal				
Date	Account/Explanation	PR	Debit	Credit
	Interest expense		171.62	
	Interest payable			171.62
	($8,000 × 9% × 87 ÷ 365)			

c.

General Journal				
Date	Account/Explanation	PR	Debit	Credit
	Note payable		8,000	
	Interest expense		65.10	
	Interest payable		171.62	
	Cash			8,236.72
	For interest expense: (8,000 × 9% × 33 ÷ 365)			

EXERCISE 12–3

a.

General Journal				
Date	Account/Explanation	PR	Debit	Credit
	Inventory (incl. prov. tax)		10,400	
	Federal sales tax recoverable		600	
	Accounts payable			11,000

b.

General Journal				
Date	Account/Explanation	PR	Debit	Credit
	Equipment (incl. prov. tax)		3,120	
	Federal sales tax recoverable		180	
	Cash			3,300

c.

General Journal				
Date	Account/Explanation	PR	Debit	Credit
	Accounts receivable..........................		17,600	
	Federal sales tax payable................			960
	Provincial sales tax payable.............			640
	Sales revenue			16,000

d.

General Journal				
Date	Account/Explanation	PR	Debit	Credit
	Cash		5,500	
	Federal sales tax payable................			300
	Provincial sales tax payable.............			200
	Sales revenue			5,000

e.

General Journal				
Date	Account/Explanation	PR	Debit	Credit
	Federal sales tax payable		1,260	
	Federal sales tax recoverable			780
	Cash			480
	For federal sales tax payable: (960 + 300)			
	For federal sales tax recoverable: (600+180)			
	Provincial sales tax payable		840	
	Cash			840
	For provincial sales tax payable: (640 + 200)			

EXERCISE 12–4

a.

General Journal				
Date	Account/Explanation	PR	Debit	Credit
	Wage expense..............................		73,000	
	Government pension expense...............		1,200	
	Government pension payable			2,200
	Tax withholding payable..................			19,000
	Employee receivable.....................			50,000
	Cash			3,000

Note: The cash represents the total of the individual payroll cheques that would be written to each employee, less the amount of the advances paid.

b.

General Journal				
Date	Account/Explanation	PR	Debit	Credit
	Wage expense.............................		36,500	
	Government pension expense...............		600	
	Accrued payroll..........................			37,100

Note:

Wage expense = 73,000 × 5 ÷ 10 = 36,500 (based on 5 working days per week)

Government pension expense = 1,200 × 5 ÷ 10 = 600

In practice, the calculation of the government pension expense would be more complicated than this. However, the company would likely omit this part of the calculation, as it is not material to the accrual.

EXERCISE 12–5

a.

	January 2016	Factor	Revenue
One-year subscription	17 × $120	12/12	$2,040
Two-year subscription	24 × $200	12/24	$2,400
Three-year subscription	30 × $280	12/36	$2,800

	July 2016	Factor	Revenue
One-year subscription	18 × $120	6/12	$1,080
Two-year subscription	20 × $200	6/24	$1,000
Three-year subscription	22 × $280	6/36	$1,027

	December 2016	Factor	Revenue
One-year subscription	12 × $120	1/12	$120
Two-year subscription	30 × $200	1/24	$250
Three-year subscription	36 × $280	1/36	$280

Total of all revenue amounts recognized = $10,997

Note: This calculation assumes that services are provided in equal proportions throughout the contract term. If a different assumption is more accurate, then the calculations would be adjusted to reflect the expected pattern of service.

b.

c.

Total contract payments received:

$$[(17 + 18 + 12) \times \$120] + [(24 + 20 + 30) \times \$200] + [(30 + 22 + 36) \times \$280] \quad = \quad \$45,080$$

Less revenue recognized in 2016	$10,997
Total deferred revenue at December 31, 2016	$34,083

This will be reported as:

Current liability	$18,013
Non-current liability	$16,070

Calculation:

	January 2016	Factor	Current Liability
One-year subscription	17 × $120	0/12	$0
Two-year subscription	24 × $200	12/24	$2,400
Three-year subscription	30 × $280	12/36	$2,800

	July 2016	Factor	Current Liability
One-year subscription	18 × $120	6/12	$1,080
Two-year subscription	20 × $200	12/24	$2,000
Three-year subscription	22 × $280	12/36	$2,053

	December 2016	Factor	Current Liability
One-year subscription	12 × $120	11/12	$1,320
Two-year subscription	30 × $200	12/24	$3,000
Three-year subscription	36 × $280	12/36	$3,360

Total current liability = $18,013

Total non-current liability = (34,083 − 18,013) = $16,070

EXERCISE 12–6

a.

General Journal				
Date	Account/Explanation	PR	Debit	Credit
Jan 1 2016	Cash		21,000,000	
	Sales revenue – yachts			20,930,000
	Unearned revenue – warranty			70,000
Dec 31 2016	Unearned revenue – warranty		23,333	
	Sales revenue – warranty			23,333
	($70,000 ÷ 3)			
Dec 31 2016	Warranty expense...........................		12,000	
	Cash			12,000
Dec 31 2017	Unearned revenue – warranty		23,333	
	Sales revenue – warranty			23,333
	($70,000 ÷ 3)			
Dec 31 2017	Warranty expense...........................		30,000	
	Cash			30,000
Dec 31 2018	Unearned revenue – warranty		23,333	
	Sales revenue – warranty			23,333
	($70,000 ÷ 3)			
Dec 31 2018	Warranty expense...........................		35,000	
	Cash			35,000

b. Unearned revenue at December 31, 2017 = $(70,000 - 23,333 - 23,333) = \$23,334$

EXERCISE 12–7

a.

General Journal				
Date	Account/Explanation	PR	Debit	Credit
	Wage expense................................		24,720	
	Accrued vacation pay			24,720
	(10 employees × $160 × 15 days × 103%)			
	Sick pay expense		15,360	
	Wage expense............................			15,360
	(96 days × $160 = $15,360)			

Note: This is simply a reclassification, as the employee would have been paid his or her regular pay on a sick day.

b. Vacation pay liability at December 31 = $24,720, per part (a)

   Sick pay liability at December 31 = $0 (these benefits do not accumulate)

EXERCISE 12–8

a.

General Journal				
Date	Account/Explanation	PR	Debit	Credit
	Cash		97,200	
	Sales revenue			92,080
	Unearned revenue – loyalty card.........			5,120

Total sales generated = 36,000 cups × $2.70 = $97,200

Fair value per cup = $97,200 ÷ (36,000 + 2,000) = $2.56 per cup

(Denominator is total cups sold plus expected redemptions.)

Unearned revenue = 2,000 expected redemptions × $2.56 = $5,120 (rounded)

General Journal				
Date	Account/Explanation	PR	Debit	Credit
	Unearned revenue – loyalty card		2,560	
	Revenue – loyalty card...................			2,560

This records the redemption of the first 1,000 free cups.

b. Liability at the end of 2015 will be the unearned revenue balance:

   = $5,120 – $2,560 = $2,560

This will be reported as a current liability, as all loyalty cards expire within one year.

EXERCISE 12–9

a.

General Journal				
Date	Account/Explanation	PR	Debit	Credit
	Factory		1,232,646	
	Obligation for site restoration.............			1,232,646

Present value of legal and constructive obligation = (FV 3,500,000, n 10, i 11%)

= $1,232,646

b.

	General Journal			
Date	Account/Explanation	PR	Debit	Credit
Year 1	Depreciation expense.......................		123,265	
	Accumulated depreciation – factory			123,265
	(1,232,646 ÷ 10 years)			
Year 1	Interest expense............................		135,591	
	Obligation for site restoration.............			135,591
	(1,232,646 × 11%)			
Year 2	Depreciation expense.......................		123,265	
	Accumulated depreciation – factory			123,265
Year 2	Interest expense............................		150,506	
	Obligation for site restoration.............			150,506
	((1,232,646 + 135,591) × 11%)			

EXERCISE 12–10

a.

	General Journal			
Date	Account/Explanation	PR	Debit	Credit
2016	Cash		33,000,000	
	Sales revenue			33,000,000
	(3,000 machines × $11,000 each)			
2016	Warranty expense..........................		1,800,000	
	Provision for warranty liability			1,800,000
	(3,000 machines × $600 per machine)			
2016	Provision for warranty liability...............		975,000	
	Cash, inventory, etc.			975,000
2017	Provision for warranty liability...............		345,000	
	Cash, inventory, etc.			345,000
2018	Provision for warranty liability...............		480,000	
	Cash, inventory, etc.			425,000
	Recovery of warranty costs			55,000

Note: This journal entry assumes that the three-year warranty period for all machines sold in 2016 has now expired. The balance of the provision must be reduced to zero once the warranty period ends. If there were still machines with remaining warranty rights, the balance of the provision would be carried forward to 2019 until the warranty period expired.

b. 2016 warranty liability = 1,800,000 − 975,000 = $825,000

2017 warranty liability = 825,000 − 345,000 = $480,000

2018 warranty liability = 480,000 − 480,000 = $0

(assuming all warranty periods have expired by the end of 2018)

Note: In 2016, the liability would be separated into current and non-current portions, based on management's best estimate of the pattern of future warranty repairs. In 2017, the liability would be reported only as current.

EXERCISE 12–11

a.

If contract is completed:

Sales revenue = 10,000 grams × $45 per gram	=	$450,000
Cost of product = 10,000 grams × $50 per gram	=	500,000
Loss on contract		$(50,000)

If contract is cancelled and sales still made:

Sales revenue (as above)		$450,000
Cost of product = 10,000 grams × $31 per gram	=	310,000
Cancellation penalty		75,000
Profit on contract		$ 65,000

If contract is cancelled and no sales made, the $75,000 penalty still applies.

Because the option of cancelling the contract and continuing to make sales results in a profit, this is not an onerous contract. No journal entry is required.

b.

If contract is completed, loss is as calculated in part (a) $ (50,000)

If contract is cancelled and sales made:

Sales revenue (as above)	$ 450,000
Cost of product = 10,000 grams × $31 per gram =	310,000
Cancellation penalty	150,000
Loss on contract	$ (10,000)

If contract is cancelled and no sales, penalty applies $(150,000)

In this case, all options result in a loss, so this is an onerous contract. A journal entry is required to recognize the least costly option available:

	General Journal			
Date	Account/Explanation	PR	Debit	Credit
	Loss on onerous contract....................		10,000	
	Provision for onerous contract			10,000

EXERCISE 12–12

a.

Ratio	2016	2015
Current	1.14	1.13
Quick	0.74	0.79
Days' sales uncollected	66 days	58 days
Days' payable outstanding	140 days	120 days

Current: 2016 $323,000 \div 284,000 = 1.14$
            2015 $294,000 \div 261,000 = 1.13$

Quick: 2016 $(323,000 - 113,000) \div 284,000 = 0.74$
           2015 $(294,000 - 88,000) \div 261,000 = 0.79$

Days' sales uncollected: 2016 $(175,000 \div 975,000) \times 365 = 66$ days
                            2015 $(150,000 \div 950,000) \times 365 = 58$ days

Days' payable outstanding: 2016 $(229,000 \div 595,000) \times 365 = 140$ days
                            2015 $(201,000 \div 610,000) \times 365 = 120$ days

b. The company's cash decreased from the previous year, but this does not reveal much. The ratio analysis, however, does reveal some worrying trends in liquidity. The current ratio has been maintained at almost exactly the same level as the previous year, but it is only slightly above 1. This may indicate that the company will have difficulty meeting its short-term obligations when they come due. The quick ratio further emphasizes this point. The quick ratio declined from the previous year and is now less than 1. This means the company would not be able to fully pay its current obligations if they were to become immediately due. This could cause problems with trade creditors and the company's bank, which could lead to further actions taken by those parties that could negatively affect the business.

The collection period for receivables has also slowed by 8 days from the previous year, which indicates that it is taking longer to collect from customers. This trend will further exacerbate any cash flow problems the company has in meeting its current payment obligations. The actual collection period of 66 days may be reasonable, but the company's credit terms and general industry conditions would need to be examined to see if this is in line with what is expected for this type of business.

The payment period for the company's suppliers shows the most alarming trend. The company is now taking 140 days to pay its payable, an increase of 20 days over the previous year. This could indicate serious cash flow problems, and may cause loss of credit with suppliers which could, ultimately, result in an inability to obtain a supply of inventory. The standard credit terms offered by suppliers will need to be examined to put this calculation into context. As well, the supplier list should be examined to see if there are any related parties involved that are granting more favourable credit terms than would be normally expected.

Overall, the company appears to have some problems in managing its working capital, which could lead to more serious liquidity problems in the future. The company seems to be using trade creditors as its main source of short term financing, which may cause a degrading of the company's credit and reputation with those suppliers. However, more information is required to fully understand these trends.

Chapter 13 Solutions

EXERCISE 13–1

a. Financing is generally obtained through three sources: borrowing the funds, issuing shares, and using internally generated funds. Using borrowed money to leverage, where the interest rate from the borrowing is less than the return from generating the profit, can maximize the returns paid to shareholders, and the related interest paid is tax deductible. However, borrowed funds must be repaid, which affects the company's liquidity and solvency risk. Issuing shares, on the other hand, does not impact liquidity and solvency risk, but it may result in the dilution of ownership and associated lower market value and less dividends per share. Using internally generated funds may be appropriate if the company has excess cash profits and has determined that this project is the best use for these funds.

b. Based on the information provided, borrowing is the most suitable source of financing for Evergreen Ltd. With a debt to total assets ratio of 56%, Evergreen Ltd. is underleveraged as compared with competitors operating in the same industry, averaging 60%. As a result, Evergreen Ltd. will likely be able to finance the expansion by borrowing and still maintain an acceptable level of liquidity and solvency risk lower than, or equal to, the 60% industry standard benchmark. If Evergreen Ltd. has significant amounts of property, plant, and equipment, it may be able to obtain the loan and secure it with its existing tangible assets. However, more information would be required before making a concrete recommendation.

EXERCISE 13–2

a.

General Journal				
Date	Account/Explanation	PR	Debit	Credit
Jan 1	Cash		400,000	
	Note payable			400,000

b.

General Journal				
Date	Account/Explanation	PR	Debit	Credit
Dec 31	Interest expense		20,000	
	Cash			20,000
	($400,000 × 5%)			

c. The market interest rate at the time of signing the note would have been 5% because the note was issued at face value, meaning that the 5% stated rate was the same as the market rate at that time.

d. The yield is the same as the market or effective rate, which is 5% in this case. Had the market rate been greater or lower than the face rate, then the yield would be equal to the market rate.

e. The current portion of the long-term debt is the principal portion of the debt that will be paid within one year of the reporting (balance sheet) date. In this case, as no principal portions are due until the note's maturity on January 1, 2019, no amount will be reported as a current portion of long-term debt as at the December 31, 2016, reporting date. However, when the balance sheet at December 31, 2018, is prepared, the long-term note payable of $400,000 will be classified as a current liability because it will be due within one year of the December 31, 2018, reporting date.

EXERCISE 13–3

a.

General Journal				
Date	Account/Explanation	PR	Debit	Credit
Jan 1	Cash		535,531	
	Bonds payable...........................			535,531
	PV = (20,000 PMT, 3.5%, 20 N, 500,000)			

b.

General Journal				
Date	Account/Explanation	PR	Debit	Credit
Jun 30	Interest expense		18,744	
	Bonds payable.............................		1,256	
	Cash			20,000
	For Interest expense: (535,531 × 3.5%)			
	For Bonds payable: (20,000 − 18,744)			
	For Cash: (500,000 × 8% × 50%)			

c.

Face value of bond	$500,000
Present value of bond	535,531
Premium	$ 35,531

EXERCISE 13–4

a.

	General Journal			
Date	Account/Explanation	PR	Debit	Credit
Jan 1	Cash		95,260	
	Note payable			95,260
	PV = (8 I/Y, 3 N, 120,000 FV)			

b.

	General Journal			
Date	Account/Explanation	PR	Debit	Credit
Dec 31	Interest expense.............................		7,621	
	Note payable			7,621
	(95,260 × 0.08)			

c. Assuming that the note face value is $120,000, the duration is three years, and the PV is equal to $95,260, then the interest rate would be:

Interest rate = (+/- 95,260 PV, 3 N, 120,000 FV) = 7.999 (or 8%)

d.

Date	Interest @ 8%	Balance
Jan 1, 2016		95,260
Dec 31, 2016	7,621	102,881
Dec 31, 2017	8,230	111,111
Dec 31, 2018	8,889	120,000

EXERCISE 13–5

a.

	General Journal			
Date	Account/Explanation	PR	Debit	Credit
Jan 1	Cash		74,326	
	Note payable			74,326
	PV = (2,400 PMT, 4 N, 5 I/Y, 80,000 FV)			

b.

	General Journal			
Date	Account/Explanation	PR	Debit	Credit
Dec 31	Interest expense.............................		3,716	
	Note payable			1316
	Cash			2,400
	For Interest expense: (74,326 × 0.05)			
	For Cash: (80,000 × 0.03)			

c.

General Journal				
Date	Account/Explanation	PR	Debit	Credit
Dec 31	Interest expense		3,819	
	Note payable			1,419
	Cash			2,400
	For Note payable: $(80,000 - 74,326) \div 4$			

EXERCISE 13–6

General Journal				
Date	Account/Explanation	PR	Debit	Credit
Jan 1, 2016	Cash		$200,000	
	Note payable			176,771
	Unearned revenue.......................			23,229
	For Note payable: PV = (2.5 I/Y, 5 N, 200,000 FV)			

EXERCISE 13–7

PMT = (+/- 25,000 PV, 3 N, 8 I/Y) = 9,700.84 (or 9,701)

Payments each December 31 would be $9,701.

EXERCISE 13–8

1.

General Journal				
Date	Account/Explanation	PR	Debit	Credit
Jan 1	Cash		324,500	
	Bond payable...........................			324,500
	$(350,000 - 25,500)$			

2.

General Journal				
Date	Account/Explanation	PR	Debit	Credit
Dec 31	Interest expense		19,200	
	Bond payable			1,700
	Cash			17,500
	For Bond payable: (25,500 ÷ 15)			
	For Cash: (350,000 × 5%)			

EXERCISE 13–9

a.

General Journal				
Date	Account/Explanation	PR	Debit	Credit
Jan 1	Cash		196,000	
	Bonds payable			196,000
	(200,000 × 0.98)			

To calculate the market rate (yield) at the time of the issuance to two decimal places:

I/Y = (+/- 196,000 PV, 7,000 PMT, 10 N, 200,000 FV) = 3.74%

General Journal				
Date	Account/Explanation	PR	Debit	Credit
Jul 1	Interest expense		7,330	
	Bond payable			330
	Cash			7,000
	For Interest expense: (196,000 × 0.0374)			
	For Cash: (200,000 × 0.07 × 6 ÷ 12)			

General Journal				
Date	Account/Explanation	PR	Debit	Credit
Dec 31, 2016	Interest expense		7,343	
	Bond payable			343
	Interest payable			7,000
	For Interest expense: ((196,000 + 330) × 0.0374)			

b.

Hobart Services Ltd.
Statement of Financial Position
as at December 31, 2016

Current liabilities:	
Interest payable	$ 7,000
Long-term liabilities:	
Long-term bonds payable, 7%, due January 1, 2021	$196,673

Check Figures:

Date	Payment	Interest @ 3.74%	Amortization	Balance	
Jan 1, 2016				196,000.00	
Jul 1, 2016	7,000.00	7,330.40	330.40	196,330.40	
Jan 1, 2017	7,000.00	7,342.76	342.76	196,673.16	← Balance owing, Dec 31, 2016
Jul 1, 2017	7,000.00	7,355.58	355.58	197,028.73	
Jan 1, 2018	7,000.00	7,368.87	368.87	197,397.61	
Jul 1, 2018	7,000.00	7,382.67	382.67	197,780.28	
Jan 1, 2019	7,000.00	7,396.98	396.98	198,177.26	
Jul 1, 2019	7,000.00	7,411.83	411.83	198,589.09	
Jan 1, 2020	7,000.00	7,427.23	427.23	199,016.32	
Jul 1, 2020	7,000.00	7,443.21	443.21	199,459.53	
Jan 1, 2021	7,000.00	7,540.47*	540.47	200,000.00	

* Rounded

Note: There is no current portion of long-term debt in this case because there is no pay-down of the principal. Looking at the payment schedule, the balance owing is increasing due to the amortization of the discount.

c.

	General Journal				
Date	Account/Explanation	PR	Debit	Credit
Jan 1	Cash		196,000	
	Bonds payable...........................			196,000
	(200,000 × 0.98)			
Jul 1	Interest expense		7,400	
	Bond payable...........................			400
	Cash			7,000
	For Bond payable: (200,000 − 196,000) ÷ 10			
	For Cash: (200,000 × 0.07 × 6 ÷ 12)			
Dec 31	Interest expense		7,400	
	Bond payable...........................			400
	Interest payable........................			7,000

d.

Hobart Services Ltd.
Statement of Financial Position
as at December 31, 2016

Current liabilities:
Interest payable $ 7,000
Long-term liabilities:
Long-term bonds payable, 7%, due January 1, 2021 $196,800

Check Figures:

Date	Payment	Interest @ 3.74%	Amortization	Balance	
Jan 1, 2016				196,000	
Jul 1, 2016	7,000.00	7,400	400	196,400	
Jan 1, 2017	7,000.00	7,400	400	196,800	← Balance owing, Dec 31, 2016
Jul 1, 2017	7,000.00	7,400	400	197,200	
Jan 1, 2018	7,000.00	7,400	400	197,600	
Jul 1, 2018	7,000.00	7,400	400	198,000	
Jan 1, 2019	7,000.00	7,400	400	198,400	
Jul 1, 2019	7,000.00	7,400	400	198,800	
Jan 1, 2020	7,000.00	7,400	400	199,200	
Jul 1, 2020	7,000.00	7,400	400	199,600	
Jan 1, 2021	7,000.00	7,400	400	200,000	

e. The total cost of borrowing will be the same for both methods, though the pattern of recognition as illustrated in the two interest schedules above is different throughout the life of the bonds.

EXERCISE 13–10

a. Effective interest rate:

$$\$800,000 \times 0.99 = \$792,000 - 7,000 = \$785,000 \text{ bond value}$$
$$\$800,000 \times 5\% = 40,000 \div 2 = 20,000 \text{ semi-annual interest payment}$$

$$I/Y = (+/- \ 785,000 \ PV, \ 20,000 \ PMT, \ 40 \ N, \ 800,000 \ FV) = 2.5756\% \text{ every 6 months}$$

Date	Payment	Interest @ 2.5756%	Amortization	Balance	
May 1, 2016				785,000*	
Jul 1, 2016	20,000	20,218	218	785,218	Bond payable balance, Dec 31, 2016
Jan 1, 2017	20,000	20,224	224	785,442	←
Jul 1, 2017	20,000	20,230	230	785,672	
Jan 1, 2018	20,000	20,236	236	785,908	
Jul 1, 2018	20,000	20,242	242	786,150	

* Fee is capitalized and will be amortized over the life of the bond. See full amortization schedule above.

b.

General Journal				
Date	Account/Explanation	PR	Debit	Credit
May 1, 2016	Cash		798,333	
	Bond payable............................			785,000
	Interest expense..........................			13,333
	For Cash: $(800,000 \times 0.99) + (800,000 \times$			
	$0.05 \times 4 \div 12) - 7,000$			
	For Bond payable: $(800,000 \times 0.99) - 7,000$			
Jul 1, 2016	Interest expense		20,218	
	Bond payable............................			218
	Cash			20,000
	For Interest expense: $(785,000 \times 2.5756\%)$			
Dec 31, 2016	Interest expense		20,224	
	Bond payable............................			224
	Interest payable..........................			20,000
	For Interest expense: $((785,000 + 2,187) \times$			
	$2.5756\%)$			
	For Interest payable: $(800,000 \times 0.05 \times 6 \div 12)$			

c.

Hobart Services Ltd.
Statement of Financial Position
as at December 31, 2016

Current liabilities:
Interest payable $ 20,000
Long-term liabilities:
Long-term bonds payable, 5%, due January 1, 2036 $785,442

d. When a note or bond is issued, the brokerage fees and any other directly attributable costs should be included in the fair value and amortized over the life of the debt. As a result, these types of additional costs will affect both the amount of the bond discount (or premium) amortized and the interest expense over the term of the bond. Exceptions to this are where the debt will subsequently be measured at fair value under the fair value option. In this case, the transaction costs would be expensed at the time of issuance and not included in the initial fair value measurement. [*CPA Handbook*, Accounting, Part II, Section 3856.07 and Part I, IAS 39.43].

EXERCISE 13–11

When a note or bond is issued, the brokerage fees and any other directly attributable costs should be included in the fair value and amortized over the life of the debt. As a result, these types of additional costs will affect both the amount of the bond discount or premium amortized and the interest expense over the term of the bond. Exceptions to this are where the debt will subsequently be measured at fair value under the fair value option. In this case, the transaction costs would be expensed at the time of issuance and not included in the initial fair value measurement. (*CPA Handbook*, Accounting, Part II, Section 3856.07 and Part I, IAS 39.43)

a. **ASPE**

	General Journal			
Date	Account/Explanation	PR	Debit	Credit
Dec 31, 2017	Interest expense		40,000	
	Cash			40,000
	($1M × 4%)			
Dec 31, 2017	Bonds payable		50,000	
	Unrealized gain			50,000
	($1M − $950,000)			

b. **IFRS (IAS 39)**

	General Journal			
Date	Account/Explanation	PR	Debit	Credit
Dec 31, 2017	Interest expense		40,000	
	Cash			40,000
	($1M × 4%)			
Dec 31, 2017	Bonds payable		50,000	
	Unrealized gain			50,000
	($1M − $950,000)			

c. The risk for Tribecca increased in this case, so the fair value of its debt owing decreased. The offsetting entry to the decrease (debit) to bonds payable is an unrealized gain. An entry booking a gain seems like an illogical outcome, given that the company is now worse off than before due to higher risk.

EXERCISE 13–12

	General Journal			
Date	Account/Explanation	PR	Debit	Credit
July 31	Bond payable		289,850	
	Loss on bond retirement		7,150	
	Cash			297,000
	For Bond payable: (300,000 − 10,150)			
	For Cash: (300,000 × 0.99)			

EXERCISE 13–13

a. Under IFRS, this debt is to be reported as a current liability on the December 31, 2016, financial statements because it was not refinanced by the reporting date. The only exception is if the refinancing was done under an agreement that existed at December 31, 2016, and the decision about the refinancing was solely up to management's discretion.

b. Under ASPE, this debt can be reported as a long-term liability because it has been refinanced on a long-term basis before the financial statements are completed. In this case, the entity's financial statements are not yet finalized, so ASPE would permit the debt to be included with long-term liabilities.

EXERCISE 13–14

Settlement or modification:

Old debt: $25,000 (amount due):

New annual interest payment: $18,000 × 6% = 1,080

New debt (PV using the old rate): PV (1,080 PMT, 8 I/Y, 3 N, 18,000 FV) = 17,072

The new debt is more than 10% difference of the old debt's value, so the renegotiation would be considered a settlement and not a modification in terms. A settlement requires the old debt to be removed from the records and the present value amount of the note payable with the new terms be recorded.

The PV of the new note payable at the current market rate would be:

PV (1080 PMT, 7 I/Y, 3 N, 18,000 FV) = 17,527.62

The entries would be:

General Journal				
Date	Account/Explanation	PR	Debit	Credit
Dec 31, 2016	Notes payable		25,000	
	Gain on restructuring of debt.............			7,472
	Note payable			17,528*
	* rounded			
Dec 31, 2017	Interest expense............................		1,227	
	Note payable			147
	Cash......................................			1,080
	For Interest expense: (17,528 × 0.07)			
	For Cash: (18,000 × 0.06)			
Dec 31, 2018	Interest expense............................		1,237	
	Note payable			157
	Cash......................................			1,080
	For Interest expense: ((17,528+147)×0.07)			
Dec 31, 2019	Interest expense............................		1,248	
	Note payable			168
	Cash......................................			1,080
	For Interest expense ((17,528+147+157)× 0.07)			
Dec 31, 2019	Note payable................................		18,000	
	Cash......................................			18,000

EXERCISE 13–15

a. Initial fair value amount of the house on January 1, 2016:

$$PV = (5.75\%, 6\ N, 800{,}000\ FV) \qquad = \quad \$572{,}015$$
$$\text{Dec 31, 2016 Interest: } (572{,}015 \times 5.75\%) \quad = \quad 32{,}891$$
$$\text{Carrying value of the note, Dec 31, 2016} \quad = \quad \$604{,}906$$

b. The assessed value for the house of $590,000 is only a tax assessment notice for purposes of tax levies and payments. Though it is intended to reflect some sort of value of the house, it may not necessarily be an accurate measure. The more accurate measure in this case would be the present value of the future cash flows of the note, using a known, agreed-upon bank rate. The tax assessment amount of $590,000 can be compared to the present value of $572,015 for consistency and reasonableness. In this case, the amounts are fairly close.

EXERCISE 13–16

a. The purchase price of the equipment should be recorded at the present value of the future cash flows of the instalment note at the imputed interest rate of 7%. This is the best measure of the fair value of the asset because it represents the present value of an agreed series of future cash flows at a known market rate. The listing price represents a tentative amount asked for the equipment and could be above or below the price that is agreed to between both parties.

b. PV = (40,541 PMT, 7 I/Y, 4 N) = 137,321

Date	Account/Explanation	PR	Debit	Credit
Jan 1	Equipment....................................		137,321	
	Note payable			137,321
Dec 31	Interest expense		9,612	
	Note payable...............................		30,929	
	Cash			40,541
	For Interest expense: (137,321 × 0.07)			

General Journal

c. From the perspective of a creditor, an instalment note payment includes both the interest and principal, whereas, for an interest-bearing note, the principal amount is not due until maturity. In other words, the instalment note provides a regular reduction of the principal balance as part of every payment received, reducing the creditor's investment in the debt and freeing up cash to use elsewhere.

EXERCISE 13–17

For Hornblower Corp.:

a. Determine if this is a modification of terms or settlement:

Present value of old debt is $700,000.

Present value of new debt using the historic rate:

PV = (45,500 PMT, 8 I/Y, 2 N, 650,000 FV) = 638,409

This loan is considered to be a modification in terms because the present value of the future cash flows of the new debt using the old rate of $638,409 does not differ by an amount greater than 10% of the present value of the old debt of $700,000.

There will be no entry for Hornblower Corp. due to the restructure of the loan. The old debt remains on the books of Hornblower Corp. at $700,000 and no gain or loss is recognized. A note disclosure regarding the modification of terms is required.

b. The interest expense is based on the future cash flows specified by the new terms with the pre-restructuring carrying amount of the debt of $700,000. The effective interest rate is calculated as follows:

I/Y = (+/- 700,000 PV, 45,500 PMT, 2 N, 650,000 FV) = 2.98% (rounded)

c.

Date	Payment	Interest @ 2.98%	Reduction in Carrying Amount	Balance
Dec 31, 2016				700,000
Dec 31, 2017	45,500	20,860	24,640	675,360
Dec 31, 2018	45,500	20,140*	25,360	650,000
		* Rounded		

General Journal				
Date	Account/Explanation	PR	Debit	Credit
Dec 31, 2017	Interest expense		20,860	
	Note payable.................................		24,640	
	Cash			45,500

d.

General Journal				
Date	Account/Explanation	PR	Debit	Credit
Jan 1, 2019	Note payable................................		650,000	
	Cash			650,000

For Firstly Trust:

e. Present value of old debt is $700,000.

Present value of new debt using the historic rate:
PV = (45,500 PMT, 8 I/Y, 2 N, 650,000 FV)   = $638,409
Loss $ 61,591

General Journal				
Date	Account/Explanation	PR	Debit	Credit
Dec 31, 2016	Bad debt expense...........................		61,591	
	Note receivable...........................			61,591

Note: If Firstly Trust had previously recorded an allowance for doubtful accounts for this note, then the debit entry would be to the AFDA account instead of the bad debt expense.

f.

Date	Payment 7%	Interest @ 8%	Reduction in Carrying Amount	Balance
Dec 31, 2016				638,409
Dec 31, 2017	45,500	51,072	5,572	643,981
Dec 31, 2018	45,500	51,519*	6,019	650,000
		* Rounded		

g.

	General Journal			
Date	Account/Explanation	PR	Debit	Credit
Dec 31, 2017	Cash		45,500	
	Note receivable		5,572	
	Interest income			51,072

h.

	General Journal			
Date	Account/Explanation	PR	Debit	Credit
Jan 1, 2019	Cash		650,000	
	Note receivable			650,000

EXERCISE 13–18

a. Determine if the changes should be accounted for as a settlement or as a modification:

Old debt: $150,000

New terms using old rate of 10%:

PV = (11,700 PMT, 10 I/Y, 2 N, 130,000 FV) = 127,744

The present value of the new terms using the old rate of 10% differs by an amount larger than 10% of the present value of the old debt of $150,000. As a result, the renegotiated debt is considered a settlement. The old debt is removed from the books of Ulting Ltd. with a gain/loss being recognized, and the new debt is recorded.

	General Journal			
Date	Account/Explanation	PR	Debit	Credit
2016	Note payable..............................		150,000	
	Gain on restructuring of debt.............			10,331
	Note payable			139,669
	PV = (11,700 PMT, 5 I/Y, 2 N, 130,000 FV)			

Interest Schedule:

Payment 9%	Interest @ 5%	Reduction in Carrying Amount	Balance
			139,669
11,700	6,983.45	4,717	134,952
11,700	6,747.62	4,952	130,000

General Journal				
Date	Account/Explanation	PR	Debit	Credit
2017	Interest expense		6,983	
	Note payable...............................		4,717	
	Cash.....................................			11,700
	For interest expense: (139,669 × 5%)			
	For Cash: (130,000 × 0.09%)			
2018	Interest expense...........................		6,743	
	Note payable..............................		4,952	
	Cash.....................................			11,700
	For interest expense: (139,669 − 4,717) × 5%			
2019	Note payable..............................		130,000	
	Cash.....................................			130,000

b.

General Journal				
Date	Account/Explanation	PR	Debit	Credit
2016	Allowance for doubtful accounts.............		22,256	
	Note receivable..........................			22,256
	($150,000 − $127,744)			

Interest schedule:

Payment 9%	Interest @ 10%	Adjust to Carrying Amount	Balance
			127,744
11,700	12,774	1,074	128,818
11,700	12,882	1,182	130,000

General Journal				
Date	Account/Explanation	PR	Debit	Credit
2017	Cash		11,700	
	Note receivable		1,074	
	Interest income			12,774
2018	Cash		11,700	
	Note receivable		1,182	
	Interest income			12,882
2019	Cash		130,000	
	Note receivable			130,000

Chapter 14 Solutions

EXERCISE 14–1

a. PV = (60,000 PMT, 8 I/Y, 4 N, 1,000,000 FV) = $933,757

b. For IFRS, the residual method is used. This allocates the proceeds first to the liability component and the residual to the equity component. The debt component is measured first as the par value compared to the present value of future cash flows without the convertible feature:

Total proceeds at par	$1,000,000
PV of the debt component by itself	(933,757)
Incremental value of option	$ 66,243

Entry:

General Journal				
Date	Account/Explanation	PR	Debit	Credit
Jan 1	Cash		1,000,000	
	Bonds payable...........................			933,757
	Contributed surplus – convertible bond options			66,243

c. Under ASPE, the zero-equity method can be used as a policy choice. The equity component would be measured at $0 and the rest to the debt component.

Entry:

General Journal				
Date	Account/Explanation	PR	Debit	Credit
Jan 1	Cash		1,000,000	
	Bonds payable............................			1,000,000

Also, the residual method can also be used as explained above. Entry is the same as the entry for IFRS:

Entry:

General Journal				
Date	Account/Explanation	PR	Debit	Credit
Jan 1	Cash		1,000,000	
	Bonds payable............................			933,757
	Contributed surplus – convertible bond options			66,243

EXERCISE 14–2

a. Under IFRS, the residual method is applied whereby cash is allocated to the value of the debt instrument first, and the residual is allocated to equity. The debt value is calculated as $576,000 and the warrants are accounted for as equity instruments.

General Journal				
Date	Account/Explanation	PR	Debit	Credit
	Cash		612,000	
	Bonds payable............................			576,000
	Contributed surplus – convertible bond options			36,000
	For Cash: (600 × $1,000 × 1.02), for Bonds payable: (600 × $1,000 × 0.96)			

b. Under ASPE one option is to measure the component that is most easily measurable first (usually the debt component) and apply the residual to the other equity component. This is the option under IFRS, and the journal entry will, therefore, be the same:

General Journal				
Date	Account/Explanation	PR	Debit	Credit
	Cash		612,000	
	Bonds payable............................			576,000
	Contributed surplus – convertible bond options			36,000
	For Cash: (600 × $1,000 × 1.02)			

Another option is to measure the equity component using the zero-equity method. This means that equity is measured at $0 and the journal entry would be:

General Journal					
Date	Account/Explanation	PR	Debit	Credit
	Cash		612,000	
	Bonds payable............................			612,000
	(600 × $1,000 × 1.02)			

c. Allocating the entire issuance to the debt component, and therefore zero to equity, results in a higher debt to total assets ratio as compared with the residual method. A lower debt to total assets ratio indicates better debt paying ability and long-run solvency.

EXERCISE 14–3

General Journal					
Date	Account/Explanation	PR	Debit	Credit
	Preferred shares.............................		80,000	
	Contributed surplus – convertible preferred shares options...............................		12,000	
	Common shares...........................			92,000
	For Preferred shares: (8,000 × $10)			

EXERCISE 14–4

a.

General Journal					
Date	Account/Explanation	PR	Debit	Credit
Jul 31	Bonds payable*.............................		648,000	
	Contributed surplus – convertible bonds** ...		90,000	
	Common shares.........................			738,000

* ($1,000,000 par value + $80,000 unamortized premium) × ($600,000 ÷ $1,000,000)

** $150,000 × ($600,000 ÷ $1,000,000)

b.

General Journal				
Date	Account/Explanation	PR	Debit	Credit
Jul 31	Bonds payable............................		400,000	
	Contributed surplus – convertible bonds.....		60,000	
	Contributed surplus – conversion rights expired......................................			60,000
	Cash......................................			400,000
	For Bonds payable: ($1,000,000 – $600,000 converted), for Contributed surplus: ($150,000 – $90,000)			

Note: The bonds payable carrying value would no longer include any unamortized premium, so the face value or par value would be the carrying value at maturity.

c. Due to common shares market price volatility, there is a risk in waiting to convert the bonds. If the bondholder does not convert when the common share market value is high, no gain will be realized. Conversely, if the common shares market price declines too far, the bondholder then risks not being able to sell the bonds, rendering the conversion rights worthless.

EXERCISE 14–5

Residual method, using the fair value of the warrants first and the residual to the bonds:

General Journal				
Date	Account/Explanation	PR	Debit	Credit
	Cash......................................		5,940,000	
	Bonds payable...........................			5,640,000
	Contributed surplus – stock warrants.....			300,000
	For Cash: ($6,000,000 × 0.99), for Bonds payable: ($5,940,000 – 300,000), for Contributed surplus: (6,000,000 ÷ 100 × $5)			

Zero-equity method, which measures the equity component at $0:

General Journal				
Date	Account/Explanation	PR	Debit	Credit
	Cash......................................		5,940,000	
	Bonds payable...........................			5,940,000

EXERCISE 14–6

Residual method:

General Journal				
Date	Account/Explanation	PR	Debit	Credit
	Cash		1,960,000	
	Bonds payable............................			1,940,000
	Contributed surplus – convertible bonds .			20,000
	For Cash: ($2,000,000 × 0.98), for Bonds payable: ($2,000,000 × 0.97)			

Zero-equity method, which measures the equity component at $0:

General Journal				
Date	Account/Explanation	PR	Debit	Credit
	Cash		1,960,000	
	Bonds payable............................			1,960,000

EXERCISE 14–7

Fair value of bonds without warrants is ($400,000 × 0.99) = $396,000

General Journal				
Date	Account/Explanation	PR	Debit	Credit
Aug 1	Cash		408,000	
	Bonds payable............................			396,000
	Contributed surplus – stock warrants.....			12,000
	For Cash: ($400,000 × 1.02)			

EXERCISE 14–8

General Journal				
Date	Account/Explanation	PR	Debit	Credit
Nov 1	Loss on redemption of bonds*...............		300,000	Must be equal
	Retained earnings**		50,000	
	Bonds payable..............................		5,650,000	
	Contributed surplus – Conversion rights.....		125,000	
	Common shares.........................			5,775,000
	Cash			350,000

* \$5,950,000 − (\$6,000,000 − \$350,000)
** \$350,000 − \$300,000

EXERCISE 14–9

Residual method:

	General Journal			
Date	Account/Explanation	PR	Debit	Credit
Sep 1, 2015	Cash		4,635,000	
	Bonds payable...........................			4,491,000
	Contributed surplus – stock warrants.....			54,000
	Interest expense.........................			90,000
	To record the issuance of the bonds.			
	For Cash: ((4,500 × \$1,000 × 1.01) + 90,000), for Bonds payable: ((4,500 × \$1,000 × 1.01) − 54,000), for Contributed surplus: (4,500 × 2 = 9,000 × \$6), for Interest expense: (\$4,500,000 × 8% × 3 ÷ 12)			

Zero-equity method:

	General Journal			
Date	Account/Explanation	PR	Debit	Credit
Sep 1, 2015	Cash		4,635,000	
	Bonds payable...........................			4,545,000
	Interest expense.........................			90,000
	For Cash: ((4,500 × \$1,000 × 1.01) + 90,000), for Bonds payable: (4,500 × \$1,000 × 1.01), for Interest expense: (\$4,500,000 × 8% × 3 ÷ 12)			

EXERCISE 14–10

a.

	General Journal			
Date	Account/Explanation	PR	Debit	Credit
Jan 1	Cash		1,500,000	
	Bonds payable...........................			1,443,138*
	Contributed surplus, conversion rights ...			56,862

* PV (10%, 5N, 135,000 PMT, 1,500,000 FV)

b.

General Journal				
Date	Account/Explanation	PR	Debit	Credit
Jan 1	Bond payable................................		1,462,697*	
	Contributed surplus, conversion rights.......		56,862	
	Loss on redemption of bonds		7,303**	
	Retained earnings		2,697***	
	Common shares.........................			1,519,559
	Cash..................................			10,000

NB: These 2 amounts must be equal to the cash payout amount of $10,000 credit.

* 1,443,138 × 10% − 135,000 = 9,314
1,443,138 + 9,314 = 1,452,452 × 10% − 135,000 = 10,245
1,452,452 + 10,245 = 1,462,697

Or: Using present values and changing the number of periods from five years to three years:

PV (10%, (5 − 2)N, 135,000 PMT, 1,500,000 FV) = $1,462,697

** 1,462,697 − 1,470,000 = 7,303
*** 10,000 − 7,303 = 2,697

EXERCISE 14–11

a.

General Journal				
Date	Account/Explanation	PR	Debit	Credit
Jan 1	Cash...		1,000,000	
	Bonds payable...........................			922,687*
	Contributed surplus, conversion rights ...			77,313

* PV(8%, 3N, 50,000 PMT, 1,000,000 FV)

b.

General Journal				
Date	Account/Explanation	PR	Debit	Credit
Jan 1	Bond payable		972,222*	
	Loss on redemption of bonds		9,240**	
	Contributed surplus, conversion rights		77,313	
	Retained earnings		41,225	
	Cash			1,100,000

* $922,687 \times 8\% = 73,815 - 50,000 = 23,815$
      $922,687 + 23,815 = 946,502 \times 8\% = 75,720 - 50,000 = 25,720$
      $946,502 + 25,720 = 972,222$

** $972,222 - 981,462 = 9,240$

EXERCISE 14–12

a. January 1, 2015: No journal entry necessary since the fair value of the forward contract would be $0.

General Journal				
Date	Account/Explanation	PR	Debit	Credit
Jan 15, 2015	Derivatives – forward contract (asset)		25	
	Gain......................................			25

b.

General Journal				
Date	Account/Explanation	PR	Debit	Credit
Jan 1, 2015	Derivatives – forward contract (asset)		20	
	Cash			20
Jan 15, 2015	Derivatives – forward contract (asset)		25	
	Gain......................................			25

EXERCISE 14–13

January 1, 2015: No entry on the grant date.

General Journal				
Date	Account/Explanation	PR	Debit	Credit
Dec 31, 2015	Compensation expense......................		100,000	
	Contributed surplus – Stock options......			100,000
	(10,000 × $20 × 1 ÷ 2)			
Dec 31, 2016	Compensation expense......................		100,000	
	Contributed surplus – Stock options......			100,000
	(10,000 × $20 × 1 ÷ 2)			
Jan 1, 2018	Cash		238,000	
	Contributed surplus – Stock options.........		140,000	
	Common shares..........................			378,000
	For Cash: (7,000 × $34), for Contributed surplus: (10,000 shares × $20 × 7,000 ÷ 10,000)			
Dec 31, 2022	Contributed surplus – Stock options.........		60,000	
	Contributed surplus – Expired stock options..			60,000
	((10,000 × $20) – 140,000)			

EXERCISE 14–14

a. January 1, 2016: No entry on the grant date.

General Journal				
Date	Account/Explanation	PR	Debit	Credit
Dec 31, 2016	Compensation expense.....................		100,000	
	Contributed surplus – Stock options......			100,000
	(200,000 × 1 ÷ 2)			
Dec 31, 2017	Compensation expense.....................		100,000	
	Contributed surplus – Stock options......			100,000
May 1, 2018	Cash		30,000	
	Contributed surplus – Stock options.........		75,000	
	Common shares..........................			105,000
	For Cash: (3,000 × $10), for Contributed surplus: ($200,000 × 3,000 ÷ 8,000)			
Dec 31, 2019	Contributed surplus – Stock options.........		125,000	
	Contributed surplus – Expired stock options..			125,000
	($200,000 – $75,000)			

b. The market price of the shares of $15 on May 1, 2018, is not used in recording the exercise of the stock options. From an accounting perspective, the market price is not relevant. It is, nonetheless, relevant to the employees in making their decision to exercise their stock options. The market price is mentioned to indicate that the timing of the exercise is justified, or at least makes sense. Employees exercising a stock option would have paid $10 and could resell the shares immediately for $15, for a gain of $5 per share.

Chapter 15 Solutions

EXERCISE 15–1

Item	Taxable Temporary Difference	Deductible Temporary Difference	Permanent Difference
A property owner collects rent in advance. The amounts are taxed when they are received.		X	
Depreciation claimed for tax purposes exceeds depreciation charged for accounting purposes.	X		
Dividends received from an investment in another company are reported as income, but are not taxable.			X
A provision for future warranty costs is recorded but is not deductible for tax purposes until the expenditure is actually incurred.		X	
Membership dues at a golf club are reported as a promotion expense but are not deductible for tax purposes.			X
Construction revenue is reported using the percentage of completion method but is not taxed until the project is finished.	X		
The present value of the costs for the future site remediation of an oil-drilling property has been capitalized as part of the asset's carrying value. This will increase the amount of depreciation claimed over the life of the asset. These costs are not deductible for tax purposes until they are actually incurred.		X	

A revaluation surplus (accumulated other comprehensive income) is reported for assets accounted for under the revaluation model. The gains will not be taxed until the respective assets are sold.	**X**		
Included in current assets is a prepaid expense that is fully deductible for tax purposes when paid.	**X**		
A penalty is paid for the late filing of the company's income tax return. This penalty is not deductible for tax purposes.			**X**

EXERCISE 15–2

	Amount
Accounting profit	$ 350,000
Permanent difference:	
Life insurance not taxable	(100,000)
Temporary difference:	
Depreciation not deductible	20,000
Taxable profit	270,000
Tax rate	20%
Current tax payable	$ 54,000

Tax expense comprised of:	
Current tax expense	$54,000
Deferred tax income (20,000 × 20%)	(4,000)
Total tax expense	$50,000

EXERCISE 15–3

a. Current Tax:

	Amount
Accounting profit	$ 3,500,000
Permanent differences:	
None	
Temporary differences:	
Construction not yet taxable	(900,000)
Capital allowance > depreciation	(1,100,000)
Taxable profit	1,500,000
Tax rate	30%
Current tax payable	$ 450,000

Temporary difference re: depreciation calculated as follows:

Cost of asset	$6,800,000
Accumulated depreciation	1,200,000
Carrying value	5,600,000
Less tax base	4,500,000
Excess capital allowance	$1,100,000

Deferred Tax Liability:

Item	Carrying Amount	Tax Base	Temp. Diff.	Rate	Deferred Tax
Construction revenue	900,000	0	(900,000)	30%	(270,000)
PPE	5,600,000	4,500,000	(1,100,000)	30%	(330,000)
Total					(600,000)

b.

General Journal					
Date	Account/Explanation	PR	Debit	Credit	
	Current tax expense		450,000		
	Current taxes payable.			450,000	
	Deferred tax expense		600,000		
	Deferred tax liability.			600,000	

c.

Profit before tax		$ 3,500,000
Income taxes		
Current expense	(450,000)	
Deferred expense	(600,000)	
		(1,050,000)
Net profit for the year		$ 2,450,000

EXERCISE 15–4

a. Current Tax:

	Amount
Accounting profit	$3,700,000
Permanent differences:	
None	
Temporary differences:	
Construction now taxable	900,000
Capital allowance < depreciation	400,000
Taxable profit	5,000,000
Tax rate	30%
Current tax payable	$1,500,000

Temporary difference re: depreciation calculated as follows:

Cost of asset	$6,800,000
Accumulated depreciation	2,600,000
Carrying value	4,200,000
Less tax base	3,500,000
Excess capital allowance	$ 700,000

Since last year's excess was $1,100,000, $400,000 of the temporary difference reversed during the year.

Deferred Tax Liability:

Item	Carrying Amount	Tax Base	Temp. Diff.	Rate	Deferred Tax
Const. rev.	0	0	0	30%	0
PPE	4,200,000	3,500,000	(700,000)	30%	(210,000)
Total					(210,000)
Opening bal.					(600,000)
Adjustment					390,000

b.

General Journal					
Date	Account/Explanation	PR	Debit	Credit	
	Current tax expense		1,500,000		
	Current taxes payable.			1,500,000	
	Deferred tax liability		390,000		
	Deferred tax income			390,000	

c.

Profit before tax		$ 3,700,000
Income taxes		
Current expense	(1,500,000)	
Deferred income	390,000	
		(1,110,000)
Net profit for the year		$ 2,590,000

EXERCISE 15–5

a. Opening deferred tax liability balance of $17,500 implies an opening temporary difference of $(17,500 \div 25\%) = \$70,000$. If the carrying amount at 31 December 2016 was $320,000, then the tax base must have been $(320,000 - 70,000) = \$250,000$.

At 31 December 2017, the carrying amount will be $(320,000 - 50,000) = \$270,000$

At 31 December 2017, the tax base will be $(250,000 - 58,000) = \$192,000$

Current Tax:

	Amount
Accounting profit	$416,000
Permanent differences:	
Non-deductible entertainment	21,000
Temporary differences:	
Warranty not deductible in 2017	56,000
Capital allowance > depreciation	(8,000)
Taxable profit	485,000
Tax rate	25%
Current tax payable	$121,250

Deferred Tax Liability:

Item	Carrying Amount	Tax Base	Temp. Diff.	Rate	Deferred Tax
Warranty	(56,000)	0	56,000	25%	14,000
PPE	270,000	192,000	(78,000)	25%	(19,500)
Total					(5,500)
Opening bal.					(17,500)
Adjustment					12,000

b.

General Journal				
Date	Account/Explanation	PR	Debit	Credit
	Current tax expense		121,250	
	Current taxes payable.			121,250
	Deferred tax liability		12,000	
	Deferred tax income			12,000

c.

Profit before tax		$ 416,000
Income taxes		
Current expense	(121,250)	
Deferred income	12,000	
		(109,250)
Net profit for the year		$ 306,750

d.

Current Liabilities	
Income taxes payable	$121,250
Non-Current Liabilities	
Deferred income taxes	5,500

EXERCISE 15–6

a. Current Tax:

	2016	2017	2018
Accounting profit	110,000	242,000	261,000
Permanent differences:			
Dividend	(10,000)	(10,000)	(10,000)
Temporary differences:			
(plug to balance)	(15,000)	(36,000)	34,000
Taxable profit	85,000	196,000	285,000
Tax rate	20%	23%	23%
Current tax payable/exp.	17,000	45,080	65,550

Deferred Tax Liability – 2016:

Item	Carrying Amount	Tax Base	Temp. Diff.	Rate	Deferred Tax
Temp Diff	15,000	0	(15,000)	20%	(3,000)
Opening bal.					0
Adjustment					(3,000)

Deferred Tax Liability – 2017:

Item	Carrying Amount	Tax Base	Temp. Diff.	Rate	Deferred Tax
Temp Diff	51,000	0	(51,000)	23%	(11,730)
Opening bal.					(3,000)
Adjustment					(8,730)

Deferred Tax Liability – 2018:

Item	Carrying Amount	Tax Base	Temp. Diff.	Rate	Deferred Tax
Temp Diff	17,000	0	(17,000)	23%	(3,910)
Opening bal.					(11,730)
Adjustment					(7,820)

b. Summary:

Income Statement

	2016	2017	2018
Current tax expense	17,000	45,080	65,550
Deferred tax expense (income)	3,000	8,730	(7,820)

Balance Sheet

	2016	2017	2018
Deferred tax liability	3,000	11,730	3,910

c.

Profit before tax	$242,000
Income taxes	
Current	45,080
Deferred resulting from temporary differences	8,280
Deferred resulting from tax rate change	450
	53,810
Net profit for the year	$188,190

Note: The deferred tax resulting from the rate change is calculated as the opening temporary difference from 2016 multiplied by the rate differential: $15,000 ×

(23% − 20%) = $450. The deferred tax resulting from temporary differences is calculated as the current year temporary differences multiplied by the current rate: $36,000 × 23% = $8,280. Deferred tax adjustments resulting from rate changes must be disclosed separately from deferred tax adjustments resulting from changes in temporary differences.

EXERCISE 15–7

a. Current Tax:

	2016	2017	2018
Accounting profit	110,000	242,000	261,000
Permanent differences:			
Dividend	(10,000)	(10,000)	(10,000)
Temporary differences:			
(plug to balance)	(15,000)	(36,000)	34,000
Taxable profit	85,000	196,000	285,000
Tax rate	20%	23%	23%
Current tax payable/exp.	17,000	45,080	65,550

Deferred Tax Liability – 2016:

Item	Carrying Amount	Tax Base	Temp. Diff.	Rate	Deferred Tax
Temp Diff	15,000	0	(15,000)	23%	(3,450)
Opening bal.					0
Adjustment					(3,450)

NOTE: Deferred tax is recorded at the rate expected to be in effect. This is substantively enacted rate at the end of 2016.

Deferred Tax Liability – 2017:

Item	Carrying Amount	Tax Base	Temp. Diff.	Rate	Deferred Tax
Temp Diff	51,000	0	(51,000)	23%	(11,730)
Opening bal.					(3,450)
Adjustment					(8,280)

Deferred Tax Liability – 2018:

Item	Carrying Amount	Tax Base	Temp. Diff.	Rate	Deferred Tax
Temp Diff	17,000	0	(17,000)	23%	(3,910)
Opening bal.					(11,730)
Adjustment					7,820

b. Summary:

	2016	2017	2018
Current tax expense	17,000	45,080	65,550
Deferred tax expense (income)	3,450	8,280	(7,820)
Deferred tax liability	3,450	11,730	3,910

c.

Profit before tax		$242,000
Income taxes		
Current	45,080	
Deferred	8,280	
		53,360
Net profit for the year		$188,640

Note: The deferred tax resulting from the rate change does not need to be reported as it was already accounted for in 2016.

EXERCISE 15–8

a.

General Journal				
Date	Account/Explanation	PR	Debit	Credit
2016	Current tax expense		2,500	
	Tax payable.............................			2,500
	(10,000 × 25%)			
2017	Current tax expense		11,000	
	Tax payable.............................			11,000
	(50,000 × 20%)			
2018	Income tax receivable.......................		13,500	
	Current tax income			13,500
	(2,500 + 11,000)			

General Journal				
Date	Account/Explanation	PR	Debit	Credit
2018	Deferred tax asset		9,400	
	Deferred tax income			9,400
	(112,000 − 55,000 − 10,000) = 47,000;			
	47,000 × 20%			
2019	Deferred tax expense		4,720	
	Deferred tax asset			4,720

(47,000 − 21,000) = 26,000 ending balance of carry forward after applying loss to reduce current taxable income to 0

Ending deferred tax = 26,000 × 18% = 4,680

Adjustment to deferred tax asset = 9,400 − 4,680 = 4,720

There is no adjustment for current taxes in 2019 because taxable income has been reduced to 0 by the carryforward.

b.

General Journal				
Date	Account/Explanation	PR	Debit	Credit
2016	Current tax expense		2,500	
	Tax payable..............................			2,500
	(10,000 × 25%)			
2017	Current tax expense		11,000	
	Tax payable..............................			11,000
	(50,000 × 20%)			
2018	Income tax receivable......................		13,500	
	Current tax income			13,500
	(2,500 + 11,000)			

No j/e in 2018 for the benefit of the loss carry forward, as the asset is not recognized. However, disclosure will be made of the unrecorded carry forward amount (47,000).

No j/e in 2019, as current tax will be 0 and no deferred tax asset will be established. However, disclosure is required of the current tax expense components:

Current tax expense 21,000 × 18%	$ 3,780
Less benefit of loss carried forward	(3,780)
Current tax expense	$ 0

As well, disclosure of the remaining, unrecorded loss carried forward (26,000) would continue.

EXERCISE 15–9

a. Current Tax:

	Amount
Accounting profit	$750,000
Permanent differences:	
Non-deductible fines	12,000
Non-taxable dividends	(7,500)
Temporary differences:	
Previously taxed revenue now earned	(95,000)
New subscriptions taxed but not earned	68,000
Capital allowance < depreciation	13,000
Taxable profit	740,500
Tax rate	30%
Current tax payable	$222,150

Deferred Tax:

Item	Carrying Amount	Tax Base	Temp. Diff.	Rate	Deferred Tax
Unearned revenue	(220,000)	0	220,000	30%	66,000
PPE	298,000	192,000	(106,000)	30%	(31,800)
Total					34,200
Opening bal.					38,400
Adjustment					(4,200)

Unearned revenue = 247,000 − 95,000 + 68,000 = 220,000
Carrying amount PPE = 357,000 − 59,000 = 298,000
Tax base PPE = 238,000 − 46,000 = 192,000

b.

	General Journal			
Date	Account/Explanation	PR	Debit	Credit
	Current tax expense		222,150	
	Current taxes payable....................			222,150
	Deferred tax expense		4,200	
	Deferred tax asset			4,200

c.

Profit before tax		$ 750,000
Income taxes		
Current expense	(222,150)	
Deferred expense	(4,200)	
		(226,350)
Net profit for the year		$ 523,650

d.

	2017	2016
Current assets		
Income taxes receivable	–	16,250
Non-current assets		
Deferred income taxes	34,200	38,400
Current liabilities		
Income taxes payable	222,150	–

EXERCISE 15–10

a. Deferred Tax Liability – 2016:

Item	Carrying Amount	Tax Base	Temp. Diff.	Rate	Deferred Tax
Temp Diff	180,000	165,000	(15,000)	25%	(3,750)
Opening bal.					0
Adjustment					(3,750)

Deferred Tax Liability – 2017:

Item	Carrying Amount	Tax Base	Temp. Diff.	Rate	Deferred Tax
Temp Diff	160,000	135,000	(25,000)	30%	(7,500)
Opening bal.					(3,750)
Adjustment					(3,750)

Deferred Tax Liability – 2018:

Item	Carrying Amount	Tax Base	Temp. Diff.	Rate	Deferred Tax
Temp Diff	140,000	135,000	(5,000)	35%	(1,750)
Opening bal.					(7,500)
Adjustment					5,750

Deferred Tax Liability/Asset – 2019:

Item	Carrying Amount	Tax Base	Temp. Diff.	Rate	Deferred Tax
Temp Diff	120,000	135,000	15,000	35%	5,250
Opening bal.					(1,750)
Adjustment					7,000

Deferred Tax Asset – 2020:

Item	Carrying Amount	Tax Base	Temp. Diff.	Rate	Deferred Tax
Temp Diff	100,000	110,000	10,000	30%	3,000
Opening bal.					5,250
Adjustment					(2,250)

NOTE: The carrying amount/tax base are determined by taking the original cost of $200,000 and deducting the accumulated depreciation/accumulated capital allowances at the end of each year.

b. Current taxes

	2016	2017	2018	2019	2020
Accounting profit (loss) reported	150,000	60,000	(440,000)	(80,000)	350,000
Temporary difference:					
Depreciation expense	20,000	20,000	20,000	20,000	20,000
Capital allowance claimed for tax purposes	(35,000)	(30,000)	0	0	(25,000)
Taxable profit (loss)	135,000	50,000	(420,000)	(60,000)	345,000
Enacted tax rate	25%	30%	35%	35%	30%
Tax payable (refund)	33,750	15,000	(48,750)*	0**	15,000***

* In 2018, a tax refund is generated as follows:

Tax loss applied to 2016 taxable profit	135,000	
Rate	25%	
Refund		33,750
Tax loss applied to 2017 taxable profit	50,000	
Rate	30%	
Refund		15,000
Total refund and tax income for the year		$48,750

** In 2019, the additional loss cannot be carried back, as there are no further taxable profits to apply it against. Therefore, no tax refund is generated.

*** In 2020, the current tax payable is determined as follows:

Taxable profit		345,000
Less loss carry forward applied:		
2018 tax loss	(420,000)	
Applied to 2016	135,000	
Applied to 2017	50,000	
2019 loss	(60,000)	
Total loss available in 2020		(295,000)
Taxable profit after loss carry forward applied		50,000
Tax rate		30%
Tax payable		15,000

c.

	2018	2019
Opening balance of loss	0	(235,000)
Current tax loss/profit	(420,000)	(60,000)
Carried back to 2016 and 2017	185,000	–
Balance to carry forward	(235,000)	(295,000)
Probability of use	80%	10%
Expected benefit	(188,000)	0
Tax rate	35%	35%
Deferred tax asset	65,800	0
Opening balance	0	65,800
Adjustment required	65,800	(65,800)

In 2019, management's estimate of its ability to utilize the tax losses has dropped to 10%, which means it is no longer probable that the asset can be realized. At this point, the asset should be derecognized.

In 2020, the balance of the loss ($295,000) can be fully used against current taxable profit ($345,000). In 2020, the company will record current tax income of $295,000 × 30% = $88,500. This will offset the current tax expense of $345,000 × 30% = $103,500, leaving a net current tax expense of $15,000. Although there is no deferred tax adjustment as the asset was previously derecognized, disclosure of the two different components of current tax expense will be required.

d.

	2016	2017	2018	2019	2020
Current tax expense (income) (from part b)	33,750	15,000	(48,750)	0	15,000
Deferred tax expense (income) – PPE (from part a)	3,750	3,750	(5,750)	(7,000)	2,250
Deferred tax (income) expense – loss (from part c)	0	0	(65,800)	65,800	0
Total tax expense (income)	37,500	18,750	(120,300)	58,800	17,250

EXERCISE 15–11

a. Current Tax:

	Amount
Accounting profit	$150,000
Permanent differences:	
None	
Temporary differences:	
Unearned rent taxed in current year	96,000
Construction revenue not taxable	(90,000)
Capital allowance > depreciation	(4,000)
Taxable income	152,000
Tax rate	30%
Current tax payable	$ 45,600

Future Tax:

Item	Carrying Amount	Tax Base	Temp. Diff.	Rate	Deferred Tax
Unearned rent revenue	(96,000)	0	96,000	30%	28,800
Construction revenue	90,000	0	(90,000)	30%	(27,000)
PPE	108,000	119,000	11,000	30%	3,300
Total					5,100
Opening bal.					4,500
Adjustment					600

NOTE: Opening balance = $(135,000 - 120,000) \times 30\% = 4,500$ DR

Summary:

Current tax expense	$(45,600)
Future tax benefit	600
Total tax expense	$(45,000)

b. Balance sheet presentation

Non-current assets	
Future income taxes	$17,700
Current liabilities	
Income taxes payable	45,600
Future income taxes	12,600

NOTE:

Non-current future tax asset $= 3{,}300 + (1 \div 2 \times 28{,}800)$

Current future tax liability $= 27{,}000 - (1 \div 2 \times 28{,}800)$

One-half of the future tax related to unearned revenue is classified as current and one-half as non-current because this is way in which the underlying unearned revenue would be classified. The future tax related to construction revenue is classified as current because the underlying construction in process account would be classified this way. The future tax related to the PPE is classified as non-current because PPE would be classified as non-current.

c.

Income Statement Presentation:

Income tax expense $(45,600)

Balance Sheet Presentation:

Current liabilities
Income tax payable $45,600

No future tax amounts are recorded.

Chapter 16 Solutions

EXERCISE 16–1

	DC or DB
The employer has no obligation to the fund beyond the required payment	DC
Accounting for this type of plan is more complicated	DB
The employer bears the investment risk with this type of plan	DB
A liability is only recorded when the required payment is not made by year-end	DC
Accounting for this type of plan will likely require the use of actuarial specialists	DB

EXERCISE 16–2

a. $10,500,000 \div 12 = \$875,000$ monthly salary
Employee contribution = $\$875,000 \times 4\% = \$35,000$
Employer contribution = $\$875,000 \times 6\% = \$52,500$

\multicolumn{5}{c}{General Journal}
Date	Account/Explanation	PR	Debit	Credit
	Pension expense...........................		630,000	
	Pension liability			87,500
	Cash (to the pension plan)..............			962,500
	Payroll expense............................		10,500,000	
	Cash (to the employees)................			10,080,000

Note:
Pension expense = $\$52,500 \times 12 = \$630,000$
Pension liability = $\$52,500 + \$35,000 = \$87,500$
Cash paid to the pension plan = $(\$52,500 + \$35,000) \times 11 = \$962,500$
Cash paid to the employees = $\$10,500,000 - (\$35,000 \times 12) = \$10,080,000$

b. The company will report a pension expense of $630,000 in the appropriate section of the income statement.

c. The company will report a pension liability of $87,500 on December 31, 2017. This will be reported as a current liability, as the funds are remitted to the plan in January 2018.

EXERCISE 16–3

a. Pension expense = $(\$832,000 - \$750,000) + \$57,000 = \$139,000$

b. Pension expense = $(\$832,000 - \$750,000) + \$57,000 - \$12,000 = \$127,000$

EXERCISE 16–4

Current Service Cost	$1,600,000
Interest on DBO	936,000
Interest on Assets	(900,000)
Pension Expense	$1,636,000

EXERCISE 16–5

a.

	Pension Plan		Company Accounting Records			
	DBO	Plan Assets	Net Defined Benefit Balance	Cash	Annual Pension Expense	OCI
Opening balance	6,300,000 CR	5,950,000 DR	350,000 CR			
Service cost	575,000 CR				575,000 DR	
Interest: DBO	441,000 CR				441,000 DR	
Interest: assets		416,500 DR			416,500 CR	
Contribution		682,000 DR		682,000 CR		
Benefits paid	186,000 DR	186,000 CR				
Remeasurement gain: assets		20,500 DR				20,500 CR
Journal entry			103,000 DR	682,000 CR	599,500 DR	20,500 CR
Closing balance	7,130,000 CR	6,883,000 DR	247,000 CR			

b.

General Journal					
Date	Account/Explanation	PR	Debit	Credit
	Pension expense............................		599,500	
	Other comprehensive income............			20,500
	Net defined benefit liability..................		103,000	
	Cash.....................................			682,000

c. The company will report a non-current liability of $247,000 on December 31, 2016.

EXERCISE 16–6

a.

	Pension Plan		Company Accounting Records			
	DBO	Plan Assets	Net Defined Benefit Balance	Cash	Annual Pension Expense	OCI
Opening balance	4,400,000 CR	4,550,000 DR	150,000 DR			
Service cost	565,000 CR				565,000 DR	
Interest: DBO	352,000 CR				352,000 DR	
Interest: assets		364,000 DR			364,000 CR	
Contribution		422,000 DR		422,000 CR		
Benefits paid	166,000 DR	166,000 CR				
Remeasurement loss: assets		52,000 CR				52,000 DR
Remeasurement loss: DBO	176,000 CR					176,000 DR
Journal entry			359,000 CR	422,000 CR	553,000 DR	228,000 DR
Closing balance	5,327,000 CR	5,118,000 DR	209,000 CR			

b.

General Journal				
Date	Account/Explanation	PR	Debit	Credit
	Pension expense............................		553,000	
	Other comprehensive income		228,000	
	Net defined benefit liability			359,000
	Cash			422,000

c.

Non-Current Liabilities:
   Net defined benefit liability $ 209,000
Accumulated Other Comprehensive Income:
   Net remeasurement losses on defined benefit liability $(228,000)

EXERCISE 16–7

a. 2015:

	Pension Plan		Company Accounting Records			
	DBO	Plan Assets	Net Defined Benefit Balance	Cash	Annual Pension Expense	OCI
Opening balance	0 CR	0 DR	0 CR			
Service cost	389,000 CR				389,000 DR	
Interest: DBO	0 CR				0 DR	
Interest: assets		0 DR			0 CR	
Contribution		348,000 DR		348,000 CR		
Benefits paid	0 DR	0 CR				
Remeasurement gain: assets		2,000 DR				2,000 CR
Remeasurement gain: DBO	27,000 DR					27,000 CR
Journal entry			12,000 CR	348,000 CR	389,000 DR	29,000 CR
Closing balance	362,000 CR	350,000 DR	12,000 CR			

Remeasurement gains are derived by working backwards from the ending balances of the DBO and plan assets. No interest is calculated as the opening balances were zero and it is assumed that transactions occur at the end of the period.

2016:

	Pension Plan		Company Accounting Records			
	DBO	Plan Assets	Net Defined Benefit Balance	Cash	Annual Pension Expense	OCI
Opening balance	362,000 CR	350,000 DR	12,000 CR			
Service cost	395,000 CR				395,000 DR	
Interest: DBO*	25,340 CR				25,340 DR	
Interest: assets**		24,500 DR			24,500 CR	
Contribution		301,000 DR		301,000 CR		
Benefits paid	50,000 DR	50,000 CR				
Remeasurement loss: assets***		15,500 CR				15,500 DR
Remeasurement loss: DBO	0 CR					0 DR
Journal entry			110,340 CR	301,000 CR	395,840 DR	15,500 DR
Closing balance	732,340 CR	610,000 DR	122,340 CR			

* $362,000 × 7% = $25,340
** $350,000 × 7% = $24,500
*** $610,000 − $350,000 − $24,500 − $301,000 + $50,000 = $15,500 CR (Work backwards from the ending balance to determine the balancing figure.)

2017:

	Pension Plan		Company Accounting Records			
	DBO	Plan Assets	Net Defined Benefit Balance	Cash	Annual Pension Expense	OCI
Opening balance	732,340 CR	610,000 DR	122,340 CR			
Service cost	410,000 CR				410,000 DR	
Interest: DBO*	58,587 CR				58,587 DR	
Interest: assets**		48,800 DR			48,800 CR	
Contribution		265,000 DR		265,000 CR		
Benefits paid	54,000 DR	54,000 CR				
Remeasurement loss: assets		15,000 CR				15,000 DR
Remeasurement loss: DBO	42,000 CR					42,000 DR
Journal entry			211,787 CR	265,000 CR	419,787 DR	57,000 DR
Closing balance	1,188,927 CR	854,800 DR	334,127 CR			

* $732,340 × 8% = $58,587
** $610,000 × 8% = $48,800

b.

2015:

General Journal				
Date	Account/Explanation	PR	Debit	Credit
	Pension expense............................		389,000	
	Other comprehensive income.............			29,000
	Net defined benefit liability................			12,000
	Cash......................................			348,000

2016:

General Journal				
Date	Account/Explanation	PR	Debit	Credit
	Pension expense............................		395,840	
	Other comprehensive income...............		15,500	
	Net defined benefit liability................			110,340
	Cash......................................			301,000

2017:

General Journal				
Date	Account/Explanation	PR	Debit	Credit
	Pension expense............................		419,787	
	Other comprehensive income...............		57,000	
	Net defined benefit liability................			211,787
	Cash......................................			265,000

c.

2015:

Non-Current Liabilities:
Net defined benefit liability (underfunded) $12,000
Accumulated Other Comprehensive Income:
Net remeasurement gains on defined benefit liability $29,000

2016:

Non-Current Liabilities:
Net defined benefit liability (underfunded) $122,340
Accumulated Other Comprehensive Income:
Net remeasurement gains on defined benefit liability $ 13,500*

* Note: Balance = $29,000 CR − $15,500 DR

2017:

Non-Current Liabilities:
Net defined benefit liability (underfunded) $ 334,127
Accumulated Other Comprehensive Income:
Net remeasurement losses on defined benefit liability $(43,500)*

* Note: Balance = $13,500 CR − $57,000 DR

EXERCISE 16–8

a.

	Pension Plan		Company Accounting Records		
	DBO	Plan Assets	Net Defined Benefit Balance	Cash	Annual Pension Expense
Opening balance	6,246,000 CR	6,871,000 DR	625,000 DR		
Past service cost	215,000 CR				215,000 DR
Service cost	510,000 CR				510,000 DR
Interest: Health Benefit Obligation*	581,490 CR				581,490 DR
Interest: assets**		618,390 DR			618,390 CR
Contribution		430,000 DR		430,000 CR	
Benefits paid	850,000 DR	850,000 CR			
Journal entry			258,100 CR	430,000 CR	688,100 DR
Closing balance	6,702,490 CR	7,069,390 DR	366,900 DR		

* ($6,246,000 + $215,000) × 9% = $581,490
** $6,871,000 × 9% = $618,390

The post-employment health benefit expense will be $688,100 for the year. Note that the interest on the health benefit obligation is calculated after taking the past service adjustment into account. This is necessary as the past service adjustment was made on January 1.

b. The company will report a non-current asset of $366,900, subject to any adjustment required as a result of the asset ceiling test.

EXERCISE 16–9

a.

	Pension Plan		Company Accounting Records		
	DBO	Plan Assets	Net Defined Benefit Balance	Cash	Annual Pension Expense
Opening balance	6,300,000 CR	5,950,000 DR	350,000 CR		
Service cost	575,000 CR				575,000 DR
Interest: DBO	441,000 CR				441,000 DR
Interest: assets		416,500 DR			416,500 CR
Contribution		682,000 DR		682,000 CR	
Benefits paid	186,000 DR	186,000 CR			
Remeasurement gain: assets		20,500 DR			20,500 CR
Journal entry			103,000 DR	682,000 CR	579,000 DR
Closing balance	7,130,000 CR	6,883,000 DR	247,000 CR		

b.

	General Journal			
Date	Account/Explanation	PR	Debit	Credit
	Pension expense...........................		579,000	
	Net defined benefit liability		103,000	
	Cash			682,000

c. The company will report a non-current liability of $247,000 on December 31, 2016.

EXERCISE 16–10

a.

	Pension Plan		Company Accounting Records		
	DBO	Plan Assets	Net Defined Benefit Balance	Cash	Annual Pension Expense
Opening balance	4,400,000 CR	4,550,000 DR	150,000 DR		
Service cost	565,000 CR				565,000 DR
Interest: DBO	352,000 CR				352,000 DR
Interest: assets		364,000 DR			364,000 CR
Contribution		422,000 DR		422,000 CR	
Benefits paid	166,000 DR	166,000 CR			
Remeasurement loss: assets		52,000 CR			52,000 DR
Remeasurement loss: DBO	176,000 CR				176,000 DR
Journal entry			359,000 CR	422,000 CR	781,000 DR
Closing balance	5,327,000 CR	5,118,000 DR	209,000 CR		

b.

General Journal				
Date	Account/Explanation	PR	Debit	Credit
	Pension expense............................		781,000	
	Net defined benefit liability			359,000
	Cash			422,000

c.

Non-Current Liabilities:
Net defined benefit liability $209,000

No accumulated other comprehensive income is reported. The remeasurement losses would simply be included in retained earnings through the closing of the pension expense account at the end of the year.

Chapter 17 Solutions

EXERCISE 17–1

a. **Lessee analysis (ASPE):**

- Does ownership title pass? No, title remains with the lessor.

- Is there a BPO or a bargain renewal option? Yes

- Is the lease term 75% or more of the asset's estimated economic or useful life? No
  6 years/10 years = 60%, which does not meet the 75% threshold

- Does the present value of the minimum lease payments exceed 90% of the leased asset's fair value? Yes, as calculated below.

Present value of minimum lease payments:
PV = (25,100 PMT/AD, 7 I/Y, 6 N, 3,000 FV) = $130,014 (rounded)

ASPE interest rate used must be the lower of the two rates, since both are known.

The present value compared to the fair value of $130,000 exceeds the 90% numeric threshold. Note that the leased asset and obligation cannot exceed fair value, so $130,000 will be the amount used as the valuation in the journal entries below.

Any one of the criteria met will result in a classification of a capital lease. In this case, the lease agreement has met two criteria: a bargain purchase option, and a present value of the minimum lease payments that exceeds 90% of the fair value of the asset.

Lessor Analysis (ASPE)

The lease agreement meets the capitalization criteria for the lessee above. Additionally, there are no uncertainties regarding the collectability of the lease payments and the costs yet to be incurred by the lessor (both must be met). This would, therefore, be classified as a capital lease for the lessor. The initial amount of net investment (fair value) of $130,000 exceeds the lessor's cost of $90,000, making the lease a sales-type lease to the lessor.

b. Gross investment (lease receivable) for the lessor:

The minimum lease payments regarding this lease are:

Calculation:	$6 \times \$25,100$	=	$150,600
BPO		+	3,000
Gross investment at inception			$153,600

Net investment for the lessor:

The $130,000 fair value in this case (or the present value if it does not exceed the fair value).

c.

	Lessee and Lessor **Lease Amortization Schedule**			
Date	Annual Lease Payment Plus BPO	Interest @ 7%	Reduction of Lease Obligation	Balance Lease Obligation
Jul 1, 2016	$ 25,100			$ 130,000
Jul 1, 2016	25,100		$ 25,100	104,900
Jul 1, 2017	25,100	$ 7,343	17,757	87,143
Jul 1, 2018	25,100	6,100	19,000	68,143
Jul 1, 2019	25,100	4,770	20,330	47,813
Jul 1, 2020	25,100	3,347	21,753	26,060
Jul 1, 2021	25,100	1,824	23,276	2,784
Jun 30, 2021	3,000	216*	2,784	0
	$153,600	$23,600	$ 130,000	

* Note: The lease valuation is limited to its fair value of $130,000 instead of the present value of $130,014. The difference ($14) is insignificant, thus a new interest rate is not required for the amortization schedule above. Had the present value been

significantly higher than the fair value, a new effective interest rate would be required and calculated using the following methodology.

I/Y = (+/- 130,000 PV, 25,100 PMT/AD, 6 N, 3,000 FV) = 7.004876% or 7%

As can be seen, the 7% rate for the lessor has not significantly changed, so 7% will be the rate used in the amortization schedule above.

d. Lessee journal entries:

General Journal				
Date	Account/Explanation	PR	Debit	Credit
Jul 1, 2016	Equipment under lease		130,000	
	Obligations under lease			130,000
	Note: Leased asset present value cannot exceed its fair value of $130,000.			
	Obligations under lease		25,100	
	Cash			25,100

Year-end adjusting entries:

General Journal				
Date	Account/Explanation	PR	Debit	Credit
Dec 31, 2016	Interest expense		3,672	
	Interest payable			3,672
	($7,343 × 6 ÷ 12 = $3,672)			
	Depreciation expense		6,425	
	Accumulated depreciation – leased equipment*			6,425
	((($130,000 − 1,500) ÷ 10 years economic life) × 6 ÷ 12)			
Jul 1, 2017	Interest payable		3,672	
	Interest expense		3,671	
	Obligations under lease		17,757	
	Cash			25,100
	For Interest expense: ($7,343 − $3,672 payable), some rounding involved			

* Note: Because there is a bargain purchase option, the leased asset is depreciated over its economic life rather than over the lease term. This is because the BPO, much less than the market price at that time, will be exercised by the lessee and the asset will be used beyond the lease term.

General Journal				
Date	Account/Explanation	PR	Debit	Credit
Dec 13, 2017	Interest expense		3,050	
	Interest payable.			3,050
	($6,100 × 6 ÷ 12)			
Dec 31, 2017	Depreciation expense.		12,850	
	Accumulated depreciation – leased equipment.			12,850
	(($130,000 – 1,500) ÷ 10 years economic life)			

e. Lessor entries

General Journal				
Date	Account/Explanation	PR	Debit	Credit
Jul 1, 2016	Lease receivable.		153,600	
	Cost of goods sold		90,000	
	Sales revenue			130,000
	Unearned interest income			23,600
	Inventory			90,000
Jul 1, 2016	Cash		25,100	
	Lease receivable			25,100

Year-end adjusting entry:

General Journal				
Date	Account/Explanation	PR	Debit	Credit
Dec 31, 2016	Unearned interest income.		3,672	
	Interest income			3,672
	($7,343 × 6 ÷ 12)			

2017 payment:

General Journal				
Date	Account/Explanation	PR	Debit	Credit
Jul 1, 2017	Cash		25,100	
	Lease receivable			25,100

Year-end adjusting entry:

General Journal				
Date	Account/Explanation	PR	Debit	Credit
Dec 31, 2017	Unearned interest income.		6,722	
	Interest income			6,722
	($7,343 × 6 ÷ 12) + (6,100 × 6 ÷ 12)			

Note: The lessor could record six months of interest income in July, and six months of interest income on December 31 to match the lessee interest entries. However, the minimum reporting requirement would be to recognize interest income each reporting date (December 31). If the lessor also had interim reporting every six months within the fiscal year, interest income would be accrued every six months to ensure that both the interim and year-end financial statements were complete.

f. For the lessee:

Rather than using quantitative factors, such as the 75% and the 90% hurdles, the IFRS criteria use qualitative factors to establish whether or not the risks and rewards of ownership have transferred to the lessee, which supports the classification as a capitalized lease:

- There is reasonable assurance that the lessee will obtain ownership of the leased property by the end of the lease term. If there is a bargain purchase option in the lease, it is assumed that the lessee will exercise it and obtain ownership of the asset (same as with ASPE).

- The lease term is long enough that the lessee will receive substantially all of the economic benefits that are expected to be derived from using the leased property over its life (equivalent to the 75% numeric threshold for ASPE).

- The lease allows the lessor to recover substantially all of its investment in the leased property and to earn a return on the investment. Evidence of this is provided if the present value of the minimum lease payments is close to the fair value of the leased asset (equivalent to the 90% numeric threshold for ASPE).

- The leased assets are so specialized that, without major modification, they are of use only to the lessee (IFRS only).

If the lease is deemed as a lease subject to capitalization, the accounting treatment of the lease by the lessee would be the same as ASPE, although it would be referred to as a finance lease, rather than a capital, direct financing lease.

The treatment of the lease by the lessor would be the same as the lessee above, using qualitative criteria rather than numeric thresholds used for ASPE. (The criteria will not include the two-revenue recognition-based tests for uncertainty regarding collectability of lease payments and estimated un-reimbursable costs for the lessor.) The lease would be referred to as a finance lease, manufacturer or dealer rather than a sales-type lease.

g. If the lease agreement included an unguaranteed residual, then the leased asset would be physically returned to the lessor at the end of the lease term. The depreciation charge would, therefore, be over the lease term and not the asset's economic life, which is the case when a bargain purchase is involved. As well, the depreciation calculation would not include a residual value.

EXERCISE 17–2

a. Lessee analysis (IFRS)

- Does ownership title pass? No, title remains with the lessor.

- Is there a BPO or a bargain renewal option? No

- Is the lease term covering the majority of the asset's estimated economic or useful life? Consider that the lease term is eight years and the economic life is ten years, so this constitutes a major part of the economic life of the asset. Yes, capitalize leased asset.

- The leased asset is a specialized piece of landscaping machinery, so it will only benefit the lessee without major modifications. Yes, capitalize leased asset.

- Does the present value of the minimum lease payments allow the lessor to recover substantially all of the leased asset's fair value as well as realizing a return on the investment? Consider that the present value of the minimum lease payments shown below is nearly equal to the fair value of $270,000, so it appears that the lessor will be reimbursed for all of the leased investment, including a return on investment. Yes, capitalize leased asset.

  Present value calculation:

Yearly payment	$46,754
Less: Executory costs	2,000
Minimum annual lease payment	$44,754

  Present value of minimum lease payments:
  PV = (44,754 PMT/AD, 9 I/Y, 8 N, 0 FV) = $269,999 (which is virtually 100% of the fair value of $270,000)

Under IFRS, the lessee will classify this lease as a finance lease since the lease term covers substantially all of the asset's useful life, the present value of the minimum lease payments allows the lessor to recover almost all of the leased asset's fair value (as well as realizing a return on the investment), and the machinery is highly specialized. Three of the criteria considered were met so it is reasonable to assume that the lessee will capitalize the lease.

The treatment of the lease by the lessor would be the same as the lessee above, using the qualitative criteria rather than numeric thresholds used for ASPE. Except the lessor classification criteria will not include the two-revenue recognition-based tests for uncertainty regarding collectability of lease payments and estimated un-reimbursable costs for the lessor. Again, since three criteria were met, it is reasonable to assume that the lease would be classified as a finance lease.

b. IFRS states that the rate implicit in the lease is to be used wherever it is reasonably determinable. Using the fair value of $270,000, the implicit rate can be calculated:

I/Y = (+/- 270,000 PV, 44,754 PMT/AD, 8 N) = 9% (rounded) which is the same rate as the lessee's

Mercy Ltd.
Lease Amortization Schedule
(Lessee)

Date	Annual Lease Payment Excluding Executory Costs)	Interest @ 9%	Reduction of Lease Obligation	Balance Lease Obligation
				$ 270,000
Jan 1, 2016	$ 44,754		$ 44,754	225,246
Jan 1, 2017	44,754	$20,272	24,482	200,764
Jan 1, 2018	44,754	18,069	26,685	174,079
Jan 1, 2019	44,754	15,667	29,087	144,992
Jan 1, 2020	44,754	13,049	31,705	113,287
Jan 1, 2021	44,754	10,196	34,558	78,729
Jan 1, 2022	44,754	7,086	37,668	41,061
Jan 1, 2023	44,754	3,693*	41,061	0
	$ 358,032	$88,032	$ 270,000	

* rounded

c.

	General Journal			
Date	Account/Explanation	PR	Debit	Credit
Jan 1, 2016	Equipment under lease		270,000	
	Obligations under lease			270,000
Jan 1, 2016	Insurance expense..........................		2,000	
	Obligations under lease....................		44,754	
	Cash			46,754
Dec 31, 2016	Depreciation expense......................		33,750	
	Accumulated depreciation–leased equipment.....................................			33,750
	($270,000 ÷ 8)			
Dec 31, 2016	Interest expense		20,272	
	Interest payable..........................			20,272
Jan 1, 2017	Insurance expense..........................		2,000	
	Interest payable............................		20,272	
	Obligations under lease....................		24,482	
	Cash			46,754
Dec 31, 2017	Depreciation expense......................		33,750	
	Accumulated depreciation–leased equipment......................................			33,750
Dec 31, 2017	Interest expense		18,069	
	Interest payable..........................			18,069

d.

Mercy Ltd.
Statement of Financial Position
December 31, 2017

Non-current assets		
Equipment under lease		$270,000
Accumulated depreciation		(67,500)
		202,500
Current liabilities		
Interest payable		18,069
Current portion of long-term lease obligation*		26,685
Non-current liabilities		
Long-term lease obligation (200,764 − 26,685)		$174,079

* The principal portion of the lease payment over the next 12 months after the reporting date of December 31, 2017. Refer to the amortization schedule above.

Required disclosure in the notes:

The following is a schedule of future minimum lease payments under the finance lease, expiring December 31, 2025, together with the balance of the obligation under finance lease.

Year ending December 31

2018	$ 46,754
2019	46,754
2020	46,754
2021	46,754
2022	46,754
2023 and beyond	46,754
	280,524
Less amount representing executory costs	12,000
Total minimum lease payments	268,524
Less amount representing interest at 9%*	67,760
Balance of the obligation, December 31, 2017	$200,764

* $88,032 total interest from schedule above − $20,272 recorded interest

Note: Additional disclosures would also be required about material lease arrangements, including contingent rents, sub-lease payments, and lease-imposed restrictions. These do not apply in this case.

EXERCISE 17–3

Lessee Analysis (IFRS)

- Does the ownership title pass? No, title remains with the lessor.

- Is there a BPO or a bargain renewal option? No

- Does the lease term cover the majority of the asset's estimated economic or useful life? Consider that the lease term is eight years, and the economic life is twelve years, the lease covers a major part of the economic life of the asset. Yes, capitalize leased asset.

- As the leased asset is a specialized piece of landscaping machinery, it will only benefit the lessee without major modifications. Yes, capitalize leased asset.

- Does the present value of the minimum lease payments allow the lessor to recover substantially all of the leased asset's fair value, as well as realizing a return on the investment? Consider that the present value of the minimum lease payments is $288,960, compared to the fair value of $300,000, making the minimum lease payments nearly equal to the fair value at that date. As such, the lessor will recover substantially all of the leased asset's fair value, as well as a return of 9% on the investment. Yes, as calculated below.

Present value calculation:

Yearly payment	$50,397
Less: Executory costs	2,500
Minimum annual lease payment	$47,897

Present value of minimum lease payments:
PV = (47,897 PMT/AD, 9 I/Y, 8 N, 0 FV) = 288,960 (which is substantially most of the fair value of $300,000)

Consider the following criteria: The lease term covers substantially all of the asset's useful life, the present value of the minimum lease payments recovers substantially most of the leased asset's fair value (as well as realizing a return on the investment), and the machinery is highly specialized for the lessee. As these three factors have been met, it is reasonable to assume that the lease will be classified as a finance lease for the lessee under IFRS.

General Journal				
Date	Account/Explanation	PR	Debit	Credit
Jan 1, 2016	Equipment under lease		288,960	
	Obligations under lease..................			288,960
Jan 1, 2016	Prepaid repair and maintenance expense ...		2,500	
	Obligations under lease....................		47,897	
	Cash			50,397
Jun 30, 2016	Depreciation expense......................		18,060	
	Accumulated depreciation – Leased equipment...................................			18,060
	($288,960 ÷ 8 × 6/12)			

General Journal				
Date	Account/Explanation	PR	Debit	Credit
Jun 30, 2016	Interest expense		10,848	
	Interest payable			10,848
	(($288,960 − 47,897) × 9% × 6 ÷ 12)			
Jun 30, 2016	Repair and maintenance expense		1,250	
	Prepaid repair and maintenance			1,250
	($2,500 × 6 ÷ 12) from Jan 1 to June 30			
Jan 1, 2017	Repair and maintenance expense		1,250	
	Prepaid repairs		1,250	
	Interest expense		10,848	
	Interest payable		10,848	
	Obligations under lease		26,201	
	Cash			50,397
	For Repair and maintenance: ($2,500 × 6 ÷ 12) from June 1 to Dec 31, 2016 For Interest expense: ($288,960 − 47,897) × 9% = 21,696 − 10,848 accrued June 30 = 10,848 interest from July 1 to Dec 31, 2016			

General Journal				
Date	Account/Explanation	PR	Debit	Credit
Jun 30, 2017	Depreciation expense		36,120	
	Depreciation − Leased equipment			36,120
06/30/17	Interest expense		9,669	
	Interest payable			9,669
	(($288,960 − 47,897 − 26,201) × 9% × 6 ÷ 12			
06/30/17	Repair and maintenance expense		1,250	
	Prepaid repair and maintenance			1,250
	($2,500 × 6/12) from Jan 1 to June 30			

EXERCISE 17–4

a. This is a finance lease to Oberton Ltd. The IFRS criteria use qualitative factors to establish whether or not the risks and rewards of ownership are transferred to the lessee, and supports classification as a finance lease:

1. There is reasonable assurance that the lessee will obtain ownership of the leased property by the end of the lease term. If there is a bargain purchase option in the lease, it is assumed that the lessee will exercise it and obtain ownership of the asset. No

2. The lease term is long enough that the lessee will receive substantially all of the economic benefits that are expected to be derived from using the leased property over its life (as evidenced by a four-year lease compared to a six-year estimated economic life). Yes, this represents a major part of the economic life of the asset.

3. The lease allows the lessor to recover substantially all of its investment in the leased property and to earn a return on the investment. Evidence of this is provided if the present value of the minimum lease payments is close to the fair value of the leased asset. Yes

    PV = (4,313 PMT/AD excl. executory costs, 8 I/Y, 4 N, 3,500 guaranteed residual) = 18,000

    Compared to a fair value of $18,000 = 100% recovery of investment + an 8% return on investment.

4. The leased assets are so specialized that, without major modification and/or significant cost to the lessor, they are of use only to the lessee. **No**

The standard also states that these indicators are not always conclusive. The decision has to be made on the substance of each specific transaction. If the lessee determines that the risks and benefits of ownership have not been transferred to it, the lease is classified as an operating lease. In this case, two factors have been met so it would be reasonable to classify this lease as a finance lease for the lessee.

For Black Ltd. (the lessor) under IFRS, the lease would receive the same treatment as for the lessee using the qualitative factors. Black Ltd. reasonably meets the factors, and is not a manufacturer or dealer, and so this is a finance lease.

b. Calculation of annual rental payment:

PMT = +/- 18,000 PV, 8 I/Y, 4 N, 3,500 FV = $4,313 + $20 executory costs = $4,333 lease payment, including executory costs of $20.

This confirms that the interest rate used to calculate the lease payment was 8% per annum.

c.

	Lease Amortization Schedule			
Date	Lease Payment Excluding Executive Costs)	Interest @ 8%	Reduction of Lease Obligation	Balance Lease Obligation
				$ 18,000
Jan. 1, 2016	$ 4,313		$ 4,313	13,687
Jan. 1, 2017	4,313	$ 1,095	3,218	10,469
Jan. 1, 2018	4,313	838	3,475	6,994
Jan. 1, 2019	4,313	560	3,753	3,241
Jan. 1, 2020	3,500	259	3,241	0
	$ 20,752	$ 2,752	$ 18,000	

d.

General Journal				
Date	Account/Explanation	PR	Debit	Credit
Jan 1, 2016	Asset under lease............................		18,000	
	Obligations under lease..................			18,000
	PV = (4,313 PMT/AD, 8 I/Y, 4 N, 3,500 FV for guaranteed residual)			
Jan 1, 2016	Obligations under lease......................		4,313	
	Insurance expense...........................		20	
	Cash.....................................			4,333
Dec 31, 2016	Interest expense............................		1,095	
	Interest payable..........................			1,095
Dec 31, 2016	Depreciation expense.......................		3,625	
	Accumulated depreciation – asset under lease....................................			3,625
	($18,000 – $3,500) ÷ 4			
Jan 1, 2017	Obligations under lease.....................		3,218	
	Interest payable............................		1,095	
	Insurance expense..........................		20	
	Cash.....................................			4,333

e.

Oberton Ltd.
Statement of Financial Position
December 31, 2016

Non-current assets		
Property, plant, and equipment		
Vehicles under lease	$18,000	
Less accumulated depreciation	3,625	
	14,375	
Current liabilities		
Interest payable	1,095	
Obligations under lease (Note 1)	3,218	
Non-current liabilities		
Obligations under lease (Note 1)	$10,469	

Note 1: The following is a schedule of future minimum payments under finance lease expiring January 1, 2020, together with the present balance of the obligation under the lease.

Year ending December 31, 2016

2017	$ 4,333
2018	4,333
2019	4,333
2020	3,500
	16,499
Amount representing executory costs	(60)
Amount representing interest	(2,752)
Balance of obligation December 31, 2016	$13,687

Oberton Ltd.
Statement of Income
for the year ended December 31, 2016

Administrative expense		
Depreciation expense	$	3,625
Insurance expense		20
Other expenses		
Interest expense		1,095

* from lease amortization schedule part (c)

f.

General Journal				
Date	Account/Explanation	PR	Debit	Credit
Jan 1, 2020	Interest payable.............................		259	
	Obligations under lease.....................		3,421	
	Accumulated depreciation...................		14,500	
	Loss on lease...............................		300	
	Asset under lease			8,000
	Cash....................................			300

g. Entries for Black Ltd.:

General Journal				
Date	Account/Explanation	PR	Debit	Credit
Jan 1, 2016	Lease receivable............................		20,752	
	Equipment acquired for lessee...........			18,000
	Unearned interest income			2,752
Jan 1, 2016	Cash.......................................		4,333	
	Insurance expense			20
	Lease receivable			4,313
Dec 31, 2016	Unearned interest income...................		1,096	
	Interest income.........................			1,095

h.

Black Ltd.
Income Statement
for the Year Ended December 31, 2016

Revenue
Interest income (leases)* $1,095

* from lease amortization schedule part (c)

Note: The insurance recovery of $20 per year would offset the original insurance expense incurred by Black Ltd.

EXERCISE 17–5

a. **Lessor Analysis (ASPE)**

The lease is a capital lease for the following reasons: the lease term exceeds 75% of the asset's estimated economic life (10 ÷ 12 years = 83%), the collectability of payments is reasonably assured, and there are no further costs to be incurred. Furthermore, it is a sales-type lease because Helmac Ltd. will realize a gross profit of $199,122 ($283,774 – $84,652) in addition to the financing charge of $75,878 to be amortized over the lease term using the effective interest method.

b.

	General Journal			
Date	Account/Explanation	PR	Debit	Credit
Jan 1, 2016	Lease receivable*............................		375,000	
	Cost of goods sold...........................		84,652	
	Sales revenue**.........................			283,774
	Inventory....................................			100,000
	Unearned interest income***.............			75,878

* (35,000 × 10 years) + 25,000 unguaranteed residual value

Note: The unguaranteed residual value is included in the lessor's gross investment even though the lessee does not guarantee it. From the lessor's perspective, it anticipates receiving $25,000 from a third party at the end of the lease term and it does not matter who they receive it from.

** The residual value is unguaranteed so its present value must be removed from the sale price to the lessee.

Present value of the minimum lease payments = (35,000 PMT/AD, 5 I/Y, 10 N, 25,000 FV) = $299,122

Sales price ($299,122 – $15,348) = $283,774 OR remove the $25,000 residual value from the present value calculation above.

PV = (35,000 PMT/AD, 5 I/Y, 10 N) = $283,774

*** The unearned interest income of $75,878 is calculated as the lease receivable (gross investment) less the present value of the minimum lease payments ($375,000 − $299,122).

General Journal					
Date	Account/Explanation	PR	Debit	Credit
May 31, 2016	Selling expense.............................		10,000	
	Cash.....................................			10,000
	(expensed per Section 3065.43)			
May 31, 2016	Unearned interest income...................		5,503	
	Interest income...........................			5,503
	((($299,122 − $35,000) × 5%) × 5 ÷ 12)			

c. Assuming the $25,000 residual value was guaranteed by the lessee, this would change the initial entry for the sale as follows:

General Journal					
Date	Account/Explanation	PR	Debit	Credit
	Lease receivable............................		375,000	
	Cost of goods sold..........................		100,000	
	Sales revenue............................			299,122
	Inventory.................................			100,000
	Unearned interest income			75,878

The sales revenue and cost of goods sold would not need to be reduced by the present value of the estimated residual value ($15,348) calculated in part (b). The sales revenue would, therefore, be the amount equalling the present value of the minimum lease payments.

d. Lease payment PMT/AD = (299,122 PV, 5 I/Y, 12 N, 40,000 FV) = $29,748 (rounded)

EXERCISE 17–6

a. Lessee Analysis (ASPE)

- Does ownership title pass? Yes, legal title passes to the lessee at the end of the lease term.

- Is there a BPO or a bargain renewal option? N/A, title passes, so BPO is not relevant.

- Is the lease term 75% or more of the asset's estimated economic or useful life? Yes

    10 years/10 years = 100% which meets the 75% threshold

- Does the present value of the minimum lease payments exceed 90% of the leased asset's fair value? Yes, as calculated below.

  Present value of minimum lease payments:

  PV = (61,507 PMT/A, 7 I/Y, 10 N, 0 FV) = $432,000 (rounded)

  The ASPE interest rate used must be the lower of the two, since both are known.

  The present value is equal to the fair value of $432,000, so it exceeds the 90% numeric threshold.

  Any one of the criteria met will result in a classification of a *capital lease for the lessee*. In this case, the lease agreement has met three criteria: legal title passes to the lessee, a lease term that exceeds 75% of the estimated economic life of the leased asset, and a present value of the minimum lease payments that exceeds 90% of the fair value of the asset.

Lessor Analysis (ASPE)

The lease agreement meets the capitalization criteria for the lessee above. In addition, there are no uncertainties regarding the collectability of the lease payments or the costs yet to be incurred by the lessor (both must be met). This would, therefore, be classified as a capital lease for the lessor. Additionally, as the lessor is a financing company this lease would be classified as a direct-financing lease by the lessor.

b. **Kimble Ltd. (lessee) entries**

	General Journal			
Date	Account/Explanation	PR	Debit	Credit
Jan 1, 2016	Cash		432,000	
	Equipment (net)			385,000
	Deferred profit on sale – leaseback			47,000
Jan 1, 2016	Equipment under lease		432,000	
	Obligations under lease..................			432,000
	(PV = (61,507 PMT/A, 7 I/Y, 10 N, 0 FV))			

Note: The present value calculation in this case will involve the annual payment (PMT) of an ordinary annuity (paid at the end of each year) for 10 periods at 7%. The interest rate under ASPE is to be the lower of the two rates, if both are known.

Earlier leasing questions involved the annual payment of an annuity due at the beginning of each year over the lease term.

General Journal				
Date	Account/Explanation	PR	Debit	Credit
Dec 31, 2016	Operating expenses.........................		7,200	
	Accounts payable (or cash)			7,200
Dec 31, 2016	Deferred profit on sale-leaseback		4,700	
	Depreciation expense....................			4,700
	($47,000 ÷ 10 years lease term)			
Dec 31, 2016	Depreciation expense......................		43,200	
	Accumulated depreciation – leased equip-ment..			43,200
	Interest expense...........................		30,240	
	Obligations under lease....................		31,267	
	Cash...................................			61,507

Note: Under ASPE, Kimble Ltd. is to use the lower of the two rates. The deferred profit on the sale-leaseback is to be amortized on the same basis that the asset is being depreciated, which, in this case, is ten years.

Quick Finance Corp. (lessor) entries

General Journal				
Date	Account/Explanation	PR	Debit	Credit
Jan 2, 2016	Equipment acquired for lease		432,000	
	Cash...................................			432,000
Jan 2, 2016	Lease receivable..........................		615,070	
	Equipment acquired for lease			432,000
	Unearned interest income			183,070
	For Lease receivable: ($61,507 × 10)			
Dec 31, 2016	Cash.....................................		61,507	
	Lease receivable			61,507
Dec 31, 2016	Unearned interest income..................		30,240	
	Interest income.........................			30,240
	(432,000 × 7%)			

Chapter 18 Solutions

EXERCISE 18–1

Transaction	Effect
Issuance of common shares	NE
Share split	NE
A revaluation of surplus resulting from a remeasurement of an available-for-sale asset	NE
Declaration of a cash dividend	D
Net income earned during the year	I
Declaration of a share dividend	D
Payment of a cash dividend	NE
Issuance of preferred shares	NE
Reacquisition of common shares	D or NE
Appropriation of retained earnings for a reserve	D
A cumulative, preferred dividend that is unpaid at the end of the year	NE

EXERCISE 18–2

	General Journal			
Date	Account/Explanation	PR	Debit	Credit
Jan 1	Cash		300,000	
	Common shares			300,000
	(20,000 × $15)			
Feb 1	Incorporation costs...........................		9,000	
	Common shares			9,000
Mar 15	Cash		500,000	
	Preferred shares			500,000
	(10,000 × $50)			
Apr 30	Equipment...................................		50,000	
	Common shares			50,000
Jun 15	Cash		125,000	
	Common shares			125,000
	(5,000 × $25)			

EXERCISE 18–3

a.

General Journal				
Date	Account/Explanation	PR	Debit	Credit
	Cash		500,000	
	Share subscription receivable		1,000,000	
	Common shares subscribed			1,500,000
	For Cash: (100,000 × $5)			
	For Share subscription: (100,000 × ($15 − $5))			

b.

General Journal				
Date	Account/Explanation	PR	Debit	Credit
	Cash		1,000,000	
	Share subscription receivable			1,000,000
	Common shares subscribed		1,500,000	
	Common shares			1,500,000

c.

General Journal				
Date	Account/Explanation	PR	Debit	Credit
	Cash		900,000	
	Share subscription receivable			1,000,000
	Common shares subscribed		1,500,000	
	Common shares			1,350,000
	Accounts payable			50,000
	For Cash: ($1,000,000 × 90%)			
	For Common shares: ($1,500,000 × 90%)			
	For Accounts payable: ($500,000 × 10%)			

d.

General Journal				
Date	Account/Explanation	PR	Debit	Credit
	Cash		900,000	
	Share subscription receivable			1,000,000
	Common shares subscribed		1,500,000	
	Common shares			1,350,000
	Contributed surplus			50,000
	For Cash: ($1,000,000 × 90%)			
	For Common shares: ($1,500,000 × 90%)			
	For Contributed surplus: ($500,000 × 10%)			

e.

General Journal				
Date	Account/Explanation	PR	Debit	Credit
	Cash		900,000	
	Share subscription receivable............			1,000,000
	Common shares subscribed		1,500,000	
	Common shares.........................			1,400,000
	For Cash: ($1,000,000 × 90%)			
	For Common shares: ($1,500,000 × 90% +			
	(100,000 × 10% × ($5 ÷ $15) × $15))			

EXERCISE 18–4

General Journal				
Date	Account/Explanation	PR	Debit	Credit
	Treasury shares............................		55,000	
	Cash			55,000
	(5,000 × $11)			
	Cash		80,000	
	Treasury shares			55,000
	Contributed surplus.....................			25,000
	For Cash: (5,000 × $16)			

EXERCISE 18–5

General Journal				
Date	Account/Explanation	PR	Debit	Credit
Jan 1	Cash		340,000	
	Common shares.........................			100,000
	Contributed surplus.....................			240,000
	For Cash: (20,000 × $17)			
	For Common shares: (20,000 × $5)			
	For Contributed surplus: (20,000 × ($17 − $5))			
Jun 30	Common shares............................		50,000	
	Contributed surplus		120,000	
	Retained earnings		20,000	
	Cash			190,000
	For Common shares: (10,000 × $5)			
	For Contributed surplus: (10,000 × ($17 − $5))			
	For Cash: (10,000 × $19)			

Note: The contributed surplus is reduced on a pro-rata basis, as this surplus resulted from a share premium on issue, and not from a previous reacquisition.

EXERCISE 18–6

	General Journal			
Date	Account/Explanation	PR	Debit	Credit
Jan 15	Cash		3,750,000	
	Common shares			3,750,000
	(150,000 × $25)			
Mar 30	Common shares		250,000	
	Contributed surplus			50,000
	Cash			200,000
	For Common shares: (10,000 × $25)			
	For Cash: (10,000 × $20)			
Jul 31	Cash		440,000	
	Common shares			440,000
	(20,000 × $22)			
Oct 31	Common shares		369,375	
	Contributed surplus		50,000	
	Retained earnings		15,625	
	Cash			435,000
	For Common shares: (15,000 × $24.625)			
	For Cash: (15,000 × $29)			

Note: Average issue cost of shares $= \dfrac{((150,000 - 10,000) \times \$25) + (20,000 \times \$22)}{160,000 \text{ shares}}$

$= \$24.625$ per share

Also, note that the contributed surplus is fully utilized because it resulted from a previous reacquisition of the same class of shares. As such, we do not need to allocate it on a pro-rata basis.

EXERCISE 18–7

General Journal				
Date	Account/Explanation	PR	Debit	Credit
May 5	Retained earnings		250,000	
	Common shares			250,000
	(100,000 × 10% × $25)			
May 15	Retained earnings		88,000	
	Dividend payable			88,000
	(100,000 × 110% × $0.80)			

May 20 – no journal entry required

General Journal				
Date	Account/Explanation	PR	Debit	Credit
May 25	Dividend payable		88,000	
	Cash			88,000
May 27	Retained earnings		660,000	
	Dividend payable			660,000
	(100,000 × 110% × 8 × $0.75)			

May 30 – no journal entry required

General Journal				
Date	Account/Explanation	PR	Debit	Credit
May 31	Dividend payable		660,000	
	Inventory			660,000
	(100,000 × 110% × 8 × $0.75)			

EXERCISE 18–8

a.

Calculation	Preferred	Common	Total
Current year: (50,000 shares × $3)	$ 150,000		$ 150,000
Balance of dividends	–	$1,050,000	1,050,000
	$ 150,000	$1,050,000	$1,200,000

b.

Calculation	Preferred	Common	Total
Arrears: (50,000 shares × $3 × 2 years)	$ 300,000		$ 300,000
Current year: (50,000 shares × $3)	150,000		150,000
Balance of dividends	–	$750,000	750,000
	$ 450,000	$750,000	$1,200,000

c.

Calculation	Preferred	Common	Total
Arrears, as before	$ 300,000		$ 300,000
Current year year basic dividend	150,000	$240,000	390,000
Current year participating dividend	196,146	313,854	510,000
	$ 646,146	$553,854	$1,200,000

Note: The basic preferred dividend is calculated as before. Then, a like amount is allocated to the common shares. The preferred dividend can be expressed as a percentage: $150,000 ÷ $5,000,000 = 3% (or $3 ÷ $100). Therefore, the common shares are also allocated a basic dividend of (3% × $8,000,000) = $240,000. This leaves a remaining dividend of $510,000, which is available for participation. The participation is allocated on a pro-rata basis as follows:

Carrying amounts of each class:

Preferred	$ 5,000,000	38.46%
Common	8,000,000	61.54%
Total	$13,000,000	100%

The participating dividend is therefore:

Preferred: $510,000 × 38.46% = $196,146
Common: $510,000 × 61.54% = $313,854

EXERCISE 18–9

a. Implied value of the company before the dividend:
5,000,000 shares × $12 = $60,000,000

50% share dividend would issue an additional 5,000,000 × 50% = 2,500,000 shares

The ex-dividend price should be $60,000,000 ÷ 7,500,000 = $8 per share

A 3-for-2 share split results in the same number of shares being issued as above, making the share price $8.

b. For the 50% share dividend, the dividend amount will be calculated as 2,500,000 × $8 = $20,000,000

Therefore, after the dividend, the equity section will appear as follows:

Common shares	$32,500,000
Retained earnings	22,000,000
Total equity	$54,500,000

A 3-for-2 share split has no effect on the accounts, as it simply increases the number of outstanding shares. Therefore, the equity section will appear as follows:

Common shares	$12,500,000
Retained earnings	42,000,000
Total equity	$54,500,000

c. Either action will result in the share price dropping to $8 per share from $12. However, the total reported equity will not change as it's just a question of how the deck will be shuffled, so to speak, in the equity section. The decision will depend on both the legal framework in the company's jurisdiction and the corporate objectives of the distribution. There may be legal restrictions and tax implications, with respect to the share dividend, which would make the share split easier to implement. On the other hand, if the directors would like to capitalize some of the retained earnings to potentially reduce future shareholder demands for dividends, then the share dividend would be the better approach. The directors will also have to consider if the shareholder response will be different for each scenario. The directors should also consider if there are any other contracts or agreements, such as loan covenants, that would be affected by the decision.

EXERCISE 18–10

a.

General Journal				
Date	Account/Explanation	PR	Debit	Credit
	Cash		45,000	
	Common shares.........................			45,000
	Common shares............................		81,250	
	Contributed surplus		7,000	
	Retained earnings		51,750	
	Cash			140,000

Average issue price = ($280,000 + $45,000) ÷ (35,000 + 5,000) = $8.125

	General Journal			
Date	Account/Explanation	PR	Debit	Credit
	Retained earnings		48,000	
	Dividend distributable			48,000
	((35,000 + 5,000 − 10,000) × 10% × $16)			
	Dividend distributable		48,000	
	Common shares			48,000
	Land		19,000	
	Preferred shares			19,000
	Retained earnings		44,000	
	Cash			44,000

Preferred dividend: (4,500 + 1,000) × $2 = $11,000
Common dividend: (35,000 + 5,000 − 10,000 + 3,000) × $1 = $33,000

b.

Ocampo Inc.
Statement of Changes in Shareholders' Equity
Year Ended 31 December 2017

	Total	Preferred Shares	Common Shares	Contributed Surplus	Retained Earnings	Accumulated Other Comp. Income
Balance on January 1	$1,217,000	$225,000	$280,000	$ 7,000	$590,000	$ 115,000
Comprehensive Income:						
Net income	120,000				120,000	
Revaluation	23,000					23,000
Total comprehensive income	143,000					
Shares issued	64,000	19,000	45,000			
Shares retired	(140,000)		(81,250)	(7,000)	(51,750)	
Cash dividend – common	(33,000)				(33,000)	
Cash dividend – preferred	(11,000)				(11,000)	
Share dividend – common	–		48,000		(48,000)	
Balance on December 31	$1,240,000	$244,000	$291,750	–	$566,250	$ 138,000

Note: Additional details of the transactions and the authorized and issued shares would be contained in the notes to the financial statements.

EXERCISE 18–11

General Journal					
Date	Account/Explanation	PR	Debit	Credit	
Jan 15	Cash		130,000		
	Treasury shares			110,000	
	Contributed surplus			20,000	

Note: Treasury shares were acquired at a price of $440,000 ÷ 40,000 = $11 per share. This is the price used to remove the treasury shares on resale.

General Journal					
Date	Account/Explanation	PR	Debit	Credit	
Feb 28	Common shares		760,000		
	Cash			705,000	
	Contributed surplus			55,000	

Average issue price = $3,800,000 ÷ 250,000 = $15.20 per share
50,000 × $15.20 = $760,000

General Journal					
Date	Account/Explanation	PR	Debit	Credit	
Jun 30	Preferred shares		625,000		
	Retained earnings		150,000		
	Cash			775,000	

Average issue price = $1,875,000 ÷ 75,000 = $25 per share
25,000 × $25 = $625,000

There is no contributed surplus balance associated with preferred share reacquisitions, so the full difference is charged to retained earnings.

General Journal					
Date	Account/Explanation	PR	Debit	Credit	
Dec 31	Retained earnings		294,500		
	Common shares			144,500	
	Cash			150,000	

Common dividend: (250,000 − 30,000 − 50,000) × 5% × $17 = $144,500

Note: The shares remaining in treasury are excluded from the dividend calculation, as the company cannot pay itself a dividend. The company's issued share capital includes the treasury shares, although they are not outstanding.

Preferred dividend: $(75,000 - 25,000) \times \$1 \times 3$ years $= \$150,000$

Note: This calculation assumes that the cumulative, unpaid dividend on the retired preferred shares was not paid. Depending on the articles of incorporation and local legislation, the cumulative, unpaid dividend may need to be paid prior to retirement of the shares. This would result in an additional dividend of $50,000 ($25,000 \times \$1 \times 2$) paid on the date of retirement.

Chapter 19 Solutions

EXERCISE 19–1

a. Basic earnings per share calculation:

Step 1: Record the opening balance of shares outstanding and each subsequent event, date, description, and number of shares for the current reporting. An event is where the outstanding number of shares changes.

Step 2: For stock dividends or stock splits, apply the required retroactive restatement factor(s) from the event point when it initially occurs and backwards to the beginning of the fiscal year.

Step 3: For each event, complete the duration between events under the date column and complete the corresponding fraction of the year column accordingly. Multiply the shares outstanding times the retroactive restatement factor(s) times the fraction of the year for each event. Sum the amounts to determine the WACS amount.

Event	Date	Description	Shares Outstanding	Retroactive Restatement Factor(s)	Fraction of the Year	Total Shares Outstanding ×Factor ×Fraction of the Year
2016						
1	Jan 1	Opening balance	100,000	2 × 1.15	2/12	38,333
	Jan 1 – Mar 1					
2	Mar 1	6,000 shares issued	6,000			
	Mar 1 – Jul 1		106,000	2 × 1.15	4/12	81,266
3	Jul 1	retired 2,000 shares	(2,000)			
	Jul 1 – Oct 1		104,000	2× 1.15	3/12	59,800
4	Oct 1	15% stock dividend	×1.15			
	Oct 1 – Dec 1		119,600	2×	2/12	39,866
5	Dec 1	10,000 shares issued	10,000			
	Dec 1 – Dec 31		129,600	2×*	1/12	21,600
6	Subsequent event	Stock split 2-for-1	×2			
			259,200			
	Total WACS				12/12	240,865

*Work restatements backwards to the beginning of the year

	Income	WACS	Basic EPS
Net income from continuing operations ($310,000 + (35,000 × 0.75))	$336,250		
Less preferred dividends	0		
Net income available to common shareholders	$336,250	240,865	$1.40

Disclosures:

Earnings per share:	Basic
Income from continuing operations	$ 1.40
Loss from discontinued operations, net of tax*	(0.11)
Net income	$ 1.29

* $35,000 × (1 − 0.25) = 26,250 ÷ 240,865

b. Common shareholders need to know how much of a company's available income can be attributed to the shares they own. This helps them assess future dividend payouts and the value of each share. Earnings per share (EPS) becomes a per share way of describing net income, making EPS a good metric for shareholders and investors. When the income statement reports discontinued operations, EPS should be disclosed for income from continuing operations, discontinued operations, and net income. These disclosures make it possible for shareholders and potential investors to know the specific impact of income from continuing operations on earnings per share, as opposed to a single EPS number, that includes income or loss from non-continuing operations not expected to continue.

c. EPS is used in the calculation of the price earnings ratio (market price of shares ÷ EPS), which compares the market price of the company's shares with income generated on a per-share basis. Market price of the company's shares will generally adjust after issuance of a stock dividend or a stock split. For the calculation of price earnings ratio to remain valid after a stock dividend or stock split, EPS should also be adjusted in the company's financial statements to assume that the additional shares have been outstanding since the beginning of the year in which the stock dividend or stock split occurred.

EXERCISE 19–2

Step 1: Record the opening balance of shares outstanding and each subsequent event, date, description, and number of shares for the current reporting. An event is where the outstanding number of shares changes.

Step 2: For stock dividends or stock splits, apply the required retroactive restatement factor(s) from the event point it when initially occurs and backwards to the beginning of the fiscal year.

Step 3: For each event, complete the duration between events under the date column and complete the corresponding fraction of the year column accordingly. Multiply the shares outstanding times the retroactive restatement factor(s) times the fraction of the year for each event. Sum the amounts to determine the WACS amount.

a.

Event	Date	Description	Shares Outstanding	Retroactive Restatement Factor(s)	Fraction of the Year	Total Shares Outstanding ×Factor ×Fraction of the Year
2016						
1	Jan 1	Opening balance	475,000	1.1	4/12	174,167
	Jan 1 – May 1					
2	May 1	25,000 shares issued	25,000			
	May 1 – Jul 1		500,000	1.1	2/12	91,667
3	Jul 1	10% stock dividend	×1.1			
	Jul 1 – Oct 1		550,000		3/12	137,500
4	Oct 1	Repurchased	(15,000)			
	Oct 1 – Dec 31	15,000 shares	535,500		3/12	133,750
	Total WACS		535,500		12/12	537,084

b.

Event	Date	Description	Shares Outstanding	Retroactive Restatement Factor(s)	Fraction of the Year	Total Shares Outstanding ×Factor ×Fraction of the Year
2016						
1	Jan 1	Opening balance	475,000	0.2	4/12	31,667
	Jan 1 – May 1					
2	May 1	25,000 shares issued	25,000			
	May 1 – Jul 1		500,000	0.2	2/12	16,667
3	Jul 1	1:5 reverse stock	×0.2			
	Jul 1 – Oct 1	split (1 ÷ 5 = 0.2)	(400,000)			
			100,000		3/12	25,000
4	Oct 1	Repurchased	(15,000)			
	Oct 1 – Dec 31	15,000 shares	85,000		3/12	21,250
		Total WACS	385,000		12/12	94,584

EXERCISE 19–3

a.

Event	Date	Description	Shares Outstanding	Retroactive Restatement Factor(s)	Fraction of the Year	Total Shares Outstanding ×Factor ×Fraction of the Year
2016						
1	Jan 1	Opening balance	500,000	3 × 1.1	1/12	137,500
	Jan 1 – Feb 1					
2	Feb 1	180,000 shares issued	180,000			
	Feb 1 – Mar 1		680,000	3 × 1.1	1/12	187,000
3	Mar 1	10% stock dividend	×1.1			
	Mar 1 – May 1		748,000	3×	2/12	374,000
4	May 1	Repurchased	(200,000)			
	May 1 – Jun 1	200,000 shares	548,000	3×	1/12	137,000
5	Jun 1	3-for-1 stock split	×3			
	Jun 1 – Oct 1		1,644,000		4/12	548,000
6	Oct 1	60,000 shares issued	60,000			
	Oct 1 – Dec 31		1,704,000		3/12	426,000
		Total WACS	1,704,000		12/12	1,809,500

b. Earnings per share:

$$\frac{\$3,500,000 - 0}{1,809,500} \text{ (declared dividend for non-cumulative preferred shares)}$$

EPS = $1.93

c. Earnings per share:

$$\frac{\$3,500,000 - (100,000 \times \$100 \times 8\%)}{1,809,500}$$ (dividend entitlement for non-cumulative preferred shares)

EPS = $1.49

d. Earnings per share:

	EPS
Income from continuing operations	$ 2.17
Discontinued operations, net of tax*	(0.24)
Net income	$ 1.93 from part (b)

* ($432,000 ÷ 1,809,500)

e. The earnings process occurs continuously throughout the fiscal year and the capital basis can fluctuate during that time. It is, therefore, necessary to adjust the denominator of the EPS ratio to reflect the various lengths of time during the year that the different amounts of capital from the different number of shares outstanding were available to generate earnings during the year.

EXERCISE 19–4

a. Basic earnings per share = $385,000 ÷ 700,000 = $0.55

Diluted EPS:

Bonds interest saved $757,232 × 6% × (1 − 0.25) × 6 ÷ 12 = $17,038

Additional shares $800,000 ÷ $1,000 × 100 × 6 ÷ 12 = 40,000 shares

Individual effect 17,038 ÷ 40,000 = $0.43 therefore dilutive

Diluted EPS = ($385,000 + 17,038) ÷ (700,000 + 40,000) = 0.5433 = $0.54

Required disclosures:

Basic EPS $0.55

Diluted EPS $0.54

b. Earnings per share = $280,000 ÷ 700,000 = $0.40

Diluted EPS:

Bonds interest saved $757,232 × 6% × (1 − 0.25) × 6 ÷ 12 = $17,038

Additional shares $800,000 ÷ $1,000 × 100 × 6 ÷ 12 = 40,000 shares

Individual effect 17,038 ÷ 40,000 = $0.43 therefore anti-dilutive

Required disclosures:

Basic and diluted EPS $0.40

Note that the company has convertible bonds, which means that it has a complex capital structure. This requires both basic and diluted EPS to be reported, even if they are the same amount.

EXERCISE 19–5

a. Follow the three steps identified earlier in the chapter to calculate the WACS in the schedule below:

Event	Date	Description	Shares Outstanding	Retroactive Restatement Factor(s)	Fraction of the Year	Total Shares Outstanding ×Factor ×Fraction of the Year
2016						
1	Jan 1	Opening balance	550,000	×2	2/12	183,333
	Jan 1 – Mar 1					
2	Mar 1	Issued shares	50,000			
	Mar 1 – Jun 1		600,000	×2	3/12	300,000
3	Jun 1	Repurchased shares	(100,000)			
	Jun 1 – Aug 1		500,000	×2	2/12	166,667
4	Aug 1	2-for-1 stock split	×2			
	Aug 1 – Dec 31		1,000,000		5/12	416,667
	Total WACS				12/12	1,066,667

Basic EPS = ($4,500,000 − 240,000)* ÷ 1,066,667 = $3.99

* (40,000 × $6) = $240,000

Note that the preferred shares are not convertible, so this company has a simple capital structure and needs only report its basic EPS.

b. The basic EPS will remain the same as the amount calculated in part (a). This is because the preferred shares are cumulative so the dividend entitlement amount would be used to reduce the income available to common shareholders. For this reason, any dividends in arrears will not be included, since they would have already been included in the previous years' respective EPS calculations. To include dividends in arrears for cumulative preferred shares in 2016 would be, in effect, double counting.

c. The basic EPS will be the same amount as calculated in part (a). If the preferred shares are non-cumulative then only dividends that are declared are deducted from net income. Since they are paid up to date, they will be the same amount as the dividend amount used in part (a), making the EPS calculation the same.

d. If the preferred shares are non-cumulative then only dividends declared would be used in the numerator to reduce net income available to common shareholders. In this case, no dividends were declared in 2016, so the calculation would be:

$$\text{Basic EPS} = (\$4,500,000) \div 1,066,667 = \$4.22$$

e. A stock split, which only increases the number of shares outstanding, will result in a decreased market price per share, making the shares more affordable to potential investors. If the company's shares are made more affordable to potential investors, then the shares may become more marketable, causing an increase in the market value as a result of the stock split.

f. The weighted average number of shares outstanding provides the correct basis for EPS to be reported because the number of common shares outstanding throughout the year can fluctuate due to various in-year capital transactions. When stock dividends or stock splits occur, a restatement of the weighted average number of shares to the beginning of the year must be made. This is done to allow valid comparisons can be made between periods before and after the stock dividend or stock split.

EXERCISE 19–6

a. This company has a complex capital structure because it has options that can potentially be converted into common shares. Both basic and diluted EPS are required to be disclosed, even if the amounts are the same.

b. Basic EPS = $350,000 ÷ 200,000 = $1.75

   Diluted EPS = $350,000 ÷ 200,000 + 4,091* = $1.71

   * Additional common shares using the treasury method:

Shares purchased	45,000
Less shares retired (45,000 × $10) ÷ $11	(40,909)
Net additional shares	4,091 shares

Note: A quick way to calculate the net additional common shares due to options (treasury method) is:

$$45,000 \text{ options} \times ((\$11 - \$10) \div \$11) = 4,091 \text{ additional shares}$$

Required disclosures:

Basic EPS	$1.75
Diluted EPS	$1.71

c. Basic EPS = $350,000 ÷ 200,000 = $1.75

   Diluted EPS = $1.75

   Options are not in the money because the market price is $9 and the exercise price is $10. Options holders would not be motivated to purchase any common shares using their options because they can buy them directly from the market at a lower price.

   Required disclosures:

   Basic and diluted EPS $1.75

EXERCISE 19–7

a. There will be no incremental shares in this case as these options are anti-dilutive. Recall that only an increase in additional shares will be dilutive since the net income (numerator) will remain unchanged. With this in mind, if call options have an exercise price ($10) that is lower than the market price ($13), these options will be anti-dilutive, as fewer shares will need to be issued (at $13) in order to obtain sufficient cash to exercise the options to purchase the 20,000 shares at $10. The net result would be a reduction of 4,615 outstanding shares, making these options anti-dilutive as calculated below:

Shares issued at $13 to obtain $200,000	15,385 increase
Using proceeds to exercise options at $10 per share	20,000 reduction

As this results in a net reduction of 4,615 common shares, these options are considered anti-dilutive and would be excluded from the diluted EPS calculation.

b.

Proceeds required to exercise options (20,000 × $14)	$280,000
Shares issued at $13 to obtain $280,000	21,538 increase
Using proceeds to exercise options at $14 per share	20,000 reduction

There is a net increase of 1,538 common shares, making this dilutive. The diluted EPS calculation would include the additional 1,538 common shares.

If the exercise price is $12 instead of $14:

Proceeds required to exercise options (20,000 × $12)	$240,000
Shares issued at $13 to obtain $240,000	18,462 increase
Using proceeds to exercise options at $12 per share	20,000 reduction

There is a net decrease of 1,538 common shares, making this anti-dilutive and, therefore, excluded from the diluted EPS calculation.

c. The company would not exercise the option to sell its common shares for $11 because the option price per share of $11 is lower than the market price of $13. These are, therefore, not dilutive.

EXERCISE 19–8

a. Basic EPS = $400,000 − 10,000* ÷ 60,000 = $6.50

* $50,000 ÷ $100 = 500 shares × $20 = $10,000 dividend annual entitlement

This company has a complex capital structure due to the convertible securities. As a result, diluted EPS is also required to be calculated and reported.

Individual effects:

4% convertible bonds:

Interest saved $97,277 × 5% × (1 − 0.24)	$3,697
Additional shares ($800,000 ÷ $1,000) × 25	20,000 shares

Individual EPS effects = $3,697 ÷ 20,000 = $0.18 (therefore dilutive)

$20, convertible preferred shares:

Dividends saved	$10,000
Additional shares (500 preferred shares × 10)	5,000

Individual EPS effects = $10,000 ÷ 5,000 = $2.00 (therefore dilutive)

Ranking:	Convertible bonds	$0.18	#1
	Preferred shares	$2.00	#2

	Income (Numerator)	Number of Shares (Denominator)	Individual EPS Effect
Basic EPS	$390,000	60,000	$6.50
4% bonds – Interest saved	3,697		
Additional shares		20,000	
Subtotal	393,697	80,000	4.92
$20 convertible preferred shares	10,000		
Additional shares ($250,000 ÷ $20) × 7 ÷ 12		5,000	
Diluted EPS	403,697	85,000	$4.75

Required disclosures:

Basic EPS	$6.50
Diluted EPS	$4.75

b. Discontinued operations gain before tax $20,000

Discontinued operations gain, net of tax ($20,000 − (1 − 0.24)) = $15,200
Net income from continuing operations = $400,000 − $15,200 = $384,800
Basic EPS, continuing operations = $384,800 − 10,000 ÷ 60,000 = $6.25

Both the bonds and preferred shares remain dilutive with the same ranking as in part (a) as they continue to be less than the basic EPS from continuing operations for $6.25, and their individual EPS effects have not changed.

	Income (Numerator)	Number of Shares (Denominator)	Individual EPS Effect
Basic EPS (from continuing operations)	$374,800	60,000	$6.25
4% bonds – Interest saved	3,697		
Additional shares		20,000	
Subtotal	378,497	80,000	4.73
$20 convertible preferred shares			
Dividends saved	10,000		
Additional shares		5,000	
Diluted EPS	388,497	85,000	$4.57

Required disclosures:

	Basic	Diluted
Income from continuing operations	$ 6.25	$ 4.57
Discontinued operations gain, net of tax*	0.25	0.18
Net income	$ 6.50	$ 4.75

* Basic ($15,200 ÷ 60,000); Diluted ($15,200 ÷ 85,000)

EXERCISE 19–9

Event	Date	Description	Shares Outstanding	Retroactive Restatement Factor(s)	Fraction of the Year	Total Shares Outstanding ×Factor ×Fraction of the Year
2016						
1	Jan 1	Opening balance	70,000	×1.1	2/12	12,833
	Jan 1 – Mar 1					
2	Mar 1	Issued shares	30,000			
	Mar 1 – Jun 1		100,000	×1.1	3/12	27,500
3	Jun 1	10% stock dividend	10,000			
	Jun 1 – Nov 1		110,000		5/12	45,833
4	Nov 1	Repurchase				
	Nov 1 – Dec 31	common shares	(20,000)		2/12	15,000
	Total WACS		90,000		12/12	101,166

Basic EPS = $350,000 − 2,000* ÷ 101,166 = $3.44

* ($2 × 1,000)

This company has convertible bonds and preferred shares so its capital structure is complex and, therefore, requires calculation and disclosure of diluted EPS.

Individual effects:

Options:

At an exercise price of $16, they are in the money.

Additional shares issued	10,000	
Shares retired (10,000 × $16 = $160,000 ÷ $18) =	8,889	
Net additional shares	1,111	dilutive

6%, convertible bonds:

Interest saved ($80,000 × 0.06 × (1 − 0.25) × 8 ÷ 12)	$2,400
Additional common shares (8,000 × 8 ÷ 12)	5,333

Individual EPS effect = $2,400 ÷ 5,333 = $0.45 (therefore dilutive)

$2, convertible preferred shares:

Dividends saved ($2 × 1,000)	$2,000
Additional shares	10,000

Individual EPS effect $2,000 ÷ 10,000 = $0.20 (therefore dilutive)

Ranking: Most to least dilutive

#1 Options   – no income effect
          – 1,111 shares

#2 Preferred shares   – income effect – $2,000
                – 10,000 shares

#3 Bonds – income effect   – $2,400
                     – 5,333 shares

	Income (Numerator)	Number of Shares (Denominator)	Individual EPS Effect
Basic EPS (from continuing operations)	$348,000	101,166	$3.44
Options		1,111	
Subtotal	348,000	102,277	3.40
Preferred shares	2,000	10,000	
Subtotal	350,000	112,277	3.12
Bonds	2,400	5,333	
Diluted EPS	$352,400	117,610	$3.00

None of the securities failed to remain dilutive so all of them will remain in the diluted EPS calculation.

Disclosures:

Basic EPS	$3.44
Diluted EPS	$3.00

Chapter 20 Solutions

EXERCISE 20–1

Description	Section	Cash Flow In (Out)
Issue of bonds payable of $500 cash	Financing	500
Sale of land and building of $60,000 cash	Investing	60,000
Retirement of bonds payable of $20,000 cash	Financing	(20,000)
Redemption of preferred shares classified as debt of $10,000	Financing	(10,000)
Current portion of long-term debt changed from $56,000 to $50,000	Financing	*
Repurchase of company's own shares of $120,000 cash	Financing	(120,000)
Amortization of a bond discount of $500	Operating	Add $500 to net income
Issuance of common shares of $80,000 cash	Financing	80,000
Payment of cash dividend of $25,000 recorded to retained earnings	Financing	(25,000)
Purchase of land of $60,000 cash and a $100,000 note (the note would be a non-cash transaction that is not directly reported within the body of the SCF but requires disclosure in the notes to the SCF)	Investing	(60,000)
Cash dividends received from a trading investment of $5,000	Operating	5,000
Increase in an available for sale investment due to appreciation in the market price of $10,000	None – non-cash gain through OCI	–
Interest income received in cash from an investment of $2,000	Operating	2,000
Leased new equipment under an operating lease for $12,000 per year	Operating	Already in net income
Interest and finance charges paid of $15,000	Operating	(15,000)
Purchase of equipment of $32,000	Investing	(32,000)
Increase in accounts receivable of $75,000	Operating	(75,000)
Leased new equipment under a finance lease with a present value of $40,000	None – non-cash	–
Purchase of 5% of the common shares of a supplier company for $30,000 cash	Investing	(30,000)

Decrease in a sales related short term note payable of $10,000	Operating	(10,000)
Made the annual contribution to the employee's pension benefit plan for $220,000	Operating	(220,000)
Increase in income taxes payable of $3,000	Operating	3,000
Purchase of equipment in exchange for a $14,000 long-term note	None – non-cash	–

* The current portion of long-term debt for both years would be added to their respective long-term debt payable accounts and reported as a single line item in the financing section.

EXERCISE 20–2

a.

Rorrow Ltd.
Balance Sheet
as at December 31, 2015

	2015	2014	Total W/C accounts except Cash*		
					Net Change
Current assets					
Cash	$ 152,975	$ 86,000			
Accounts receivable (net)	321,640	239,080			
Inventory	801,410	855,700	1,160,890	1,124,880	(36,010)
Prepaid insurance expenses	37,840	30,100			
Equipment	2,564,950	2,156,450			
Accumulated depreciation, equipment	(625,220)	(524,600)			
Total assets	$3,253,595	$2,842,730			
Current liabilities					
Accounts payable	$ 478,900	$ 494,500			
Salaries and wages payable	312,300	309,600	897,410	901,280	(3,870)
Accrued interest payable	106,210	97,180			
Bonds payable, due July 31, 2023	322,500	430,000			
Common shares	1,509,300	1,204,000			
Retained earnings	524,385	307,450			
Total liabilities and shareholders' equity	$3,253,595	2,842,730		Net change	(39,880)

* exclude current portion of long-term debt as this account is not a working capital account

Rorrow Ltd.
Income Statement
For the year ended December 31, 2015

Sales	$ 5,258,246
Expenses	
Cost of goods sold	3,150,180
Salaries and benefits expense	754,186
Depreciation expense	100,620
Interest expense	258,129
Insurance expense	95,976
Income tax expense	253,098
	4,612,189
Net income	$ 646,057

Rorrow Ltd.
SCF - Direct Method Worksheet

	I/S Accounts	Changes to Working Capital Accounts	Net Cash Flow In (Out)
Cash received from sales	$ 5,258,246	$ (82,560)	$ 5,175,686
Cash paid for goods and services	(3,150,180)	54,290	
	(95,976)	(7,740)	
		(15,600)	(3,215,206)
Cash paid to or on behalf of employees	(754,186)	2,700	(751,486)
Cash paid for interest	(258,129)	9,030	(249,099)
Cash paid for income taxes	(253,098)		(253,098)
Memo items:			
Depreciation expense	(100,620)		
Net cash flows from operating activities	$ 646,057	$ (39,880)	$ 706,797

This amount balances to net change in W/C accounts shown above

b.

Rorrow Ltd.
Statement of Cash Flows – Operating Activities
For the year ended December 31, 2015

Cash flows from operating activities	
Cash received from sales	$5,175,686
Cash paid for goods and services	3,215,206
Cash paid to or on behalf of employees	751,486
Cash paid for interest	249,099
Cash paid for income taxes	253,098
Net cash flows from operating activities	$ 706,797

EXERCISE 20–3

a.

Carmel Corp.
Statement of Cash Flows
For the year ended December 31, 2016

Cash flows from operating activities		
Net income		$105,000
Adjustments for non-cash revenue and expense items in the income statement:		
Depreciation expense	$ 48,000	
Gain on sale of investments	(2,200)	
Loss on sale of building	5,000	
Decrease in investments – trading	136,600	
Increase in accounts receivable ($109,040 – $89,040)	(20,000)	
Decrease in accounts payable ($146,000 – $55,200)	(90,800)	76,600
Net cash from operating activities		181,600
Cash flows from investing activities		
Proceeds from sale of building ($225,000 – $5,000)	220,000	
Purchase of land	(220,000)	
Net cash from investing activities		0
Cash flows from financing activities		
Reduction in long-term mortgage principal	(30,000)	
Issuance of common shares	20,000	
Payment of cash dividends	(8,000)	
Net cash from financing activities		(18,000)
Net increase in cash		163,600
Cash at beginning of year		84,000
Cash at end of year		$247,600

Supplemental Disclosures:

1. The purchase of equipment through the issuance of $50,000 of common shares is a significant non-cash financing transaction that would be disclosed in the notes to the financial statements.

Cash paid interest $35,000

2. Note: Had there been cash paid income taxes, this would also be disclosed.

b. Free cash flow:

Net cash from operating activities	$ 181,600
Capital expenditures – land	(220,000)
Cash paid dividends	(8,000)
Free cash flow	$ (46,400)

In the analysis of Carmel's free cash flow above, we see that it is negative. While including dividends paid is optional, it would not have made a difference in this case. What does make a difference, however, is that the capital expenditures are those needed to sustain the current level of operations. In the case of Carmel Corp., the land was purchased for investment purposes, and not to meet operational requirements. With this in mind, the free cash flow would more accurately be:

Net cash from operating activities	$181,600
Capital purchases	0
Cash paid dividends	(8,000)
Free cash flow	$173,600

This makes intuitive sense and it is supported by the results from one of the coverage ratios.

The current cash debt coverage provides information about how well Carmel Corp. can cover its current liabilities from its net cash flows from operations:

$$\frac{\text{Net cash from operating activities}}{\text{Average current liabilities}}$$

Carmel Corp.'s current cash debt coverage is 1.38 ($181,600÷((87,200+176,000)× 50%)). The company has adequate cash flows to cover its current liabilities as they come due and so, overall, its financial flexibility looks positive.

In terms of cash flow patterns, we see a positive trend, as Carmel Corp. has managed to more than triple its cash balance in the year, mainly from cash generated from operating activities. They were able to pay $8,000 in dividends, or a 1.7% return. And if dividends are paid several times throughout the year, then the return is more than adequate for investors. Carmel Corp. also sold off its traded investments for a profit, and some idle buildings at a small loss, to obtain sufficient internal funding for some land that they want to purchase as an investment. They also managed to lower their accounts payable levels by close to 60%. All of this supports the assessment that Carmel Corp.'s financial flexibility looks reasonable.

c. The information reported in the statement of cash flows is useful for assessing the amount, timing, and uncertainty of future cash flows. The statement identifies the specific cash inflows and outflows from operating activities, investing activities, and financing activities. This gives stakeholders a better understanding of the liquidity and financial flexibility of the enterprise. Some stakeholders have concerns about the quality of the earnings because of the variety and subjectivity of the bases that can be used to record accruals and estimates. As a result, the higher the ratio of cash provided by operating activities to net income, the more stakeholders can rely on the earnings reported.

EXERCISE 20–4

Lambrinetta Industries Ltd.
Statement of Cash Flows
Year Ended December 31, 2016

Cash flows from operating activities		
Net income		$ 161,500
Adjustments		
Depreciation expense*	$ 25,500	
Change in A/R	27,200	
Change in A/P	11,900	
Unrealized loss on investments – trading**	5,200	
		69,800
Net cash from operating activities		231,300
Cash flows from investing activities		
Sold plant assets	37,400	
Purchase plant assets***	(130,900)	
Investments purchased	(12,000)	
Net cash from investing activities		(105,500)
Cash flows from financing activities		
Note issued****	42,500	
Shares issued for cash		
(81,600 + 37,400 in exch for land –		
130,900 ending balance)	11,900	
Cash dividends paid*****	(188,700)	
Net cash from financing activities		(134,300)
Net decrease in cash		(8,500)
Cash at beginning of year		40,800
Cash at end of year		$ 32,300

* $136,000 − $13,600 − $147,900

** $81,600 + $12,000 − $88,400

*** $345,100 − $51,000 − $425,000

**** $75,000 + $10,000 − $119,500 − $8,000

***** $314,500 + $161,500 − $287,300

Disclosures:

Additional land for $37,400 was acquired in exchange for issuing additional common shares.

EXERCISE 20–5

a.

Egglestone Vibe Inc.
Statement of Cash Flows
For the year ended December 31, 2016

Cash flows from operating activities		
Net income		$ 24,700
Adjustments to reconcile net income to		
net cash provided by operating activities		
Depreciation expense (note 1)	$ 55,900	
Loss on sale of equipment (note 2)	10,100	
Gain on sale of land (note 3)	(38,200)	
Impairment loss – goodwill	63,700	
Increase in accounts receivable	(36,400)	
Increase in inventory	(67,600)	
Decrease in accounts payable	(28,200)	(40,700)
Net cash used by operating activities		(16,000)
Cash flows from investing activities		
Purchase of investments – available for sale	(20,000)	
Proceeds from sale of equipment	27,300	
Purchase of land (note 4)	(62,400)	
Proceeds from sale of land	150,000	
Net cash provided by investing activities		94,900
Cash flows used by financing activities		
Payment of cash dividends (note 5)	(42,600)	
Issuance of notes payable	10,500	
Net cash used by financing activities		(32,100)
Net increase in cash		46,800
Cash at beginning of year		37,700
Cash at end of year		$ 84,500

General note: During the year, Egglestone Vibe retired $160,000 in notes payable by issuing common shares.

Notes to statements:

1. $111,800 − $15,600 + X = $152,100; X = $55,900

2. $27,300 − ($53,000 − $15,600)

3. $150,000 − $111,800

4. $133,900 − 111,800 + X = $84,500

5. Retained earnings account: $370,200 + $24,700 − X = $374,400; Dividend declared but not paid = $20,500

   Dividends payable account: $41,600 + $20,500 − $19,500 = $42,600 cash paid dividends

b. Negative cash flows from operating activities may signal trouble ahead with regard to Egglestone's daily operations, including profitability of operations and management of its current assets, such as accounts receivable, inventory and accounts payable. All three of these increased the cash outflows over the year. In fact, net cash provided by investing activities funded the net cash used by both operating and financing activities. Specifically, proceeds from sale of equipment and land were used to fund operating and financing activities, which may be cause for concern if the assets sold were used to generate significant revenue. Shareholders did receive cash dividends, but investors may wonder if these payments will be sustainable over the long term. Consider that dividends declared were $20,500, which was quite high compared to the net income of $24,700. In addition, the dividends payable account still had a balance payable of $41,600 from prior dividend declarations not yet paid. This creates increased pressure on the company to find sufficient funds to catch-up with the cash payments owed to investors. Egglestone may not be able to sustain payment of cash dividends of this size in the long-term if improvement of its profitability and management of its receivables, payables, and inventory are not implemented quickly.

EXERCISE 20–6

a. For operating activities, use the steps from earlier in the chapter for the direct method:

Step 3 – enter all the line items from the income statement to the most appropriate direct method category so that the total matches the income statement.

Step 4 – enter all the changes to the non-cash working capital accounts (except current portion of LT debt) to the most appropriate direct method category, and use the accounting equation technique to determine if the cash flow change for each account is positive or negative.

Complete the investing and financing sections as usual.

Bognar Ltd.
Statement of Cash Flows Worksheet – Direct Method
For the year ended December 31, 2015

	Step 3	Step 4	Step 5
		Changes to W/C +/- add'l	Net
Cash flows from operating activities:	I/S Accounts	adjustments	cash flow
Cash received from sales – Sales	$ 1,852,400		
– Accounts receivable		$ (108,000)	$ 1,744,400
Cash paid for goods and services – COGS	(1,213,300)		
– Other operating expenses	(342,100)		
– Inventory		(146,000)	
– Accounts payable		(37,300)	(1,738,700)
Cash paid to employees			N/A
Cash received for interest income			0
Cash paid for interest for Bonds payable, net of discount ($1,034,250 – 1,089,000) = $54,750 non-cash interest expense	(126,500)	54,750*	(71,750)
Cash received for income taxes ($69,300 – 26,400)	59,400	(42,900)**	16,500
Cash received for dividends			0
Memo Items:			
Depreciation	(121,000)		
Depreciation	(82,500)		
Goodwill impairment	(66,000)		
Loss on Held for Trading investments	(32,500)	32,500***	
Gain on sale of land	24,200		
Loss on sale of machine	(10,800)		
Net cash flows from operating activities	(58,700)		(49,550)

Cash flows from investing activities:	
Proceeds from sale of land ($430,500 – 363,000 + 24,200 gain	91,700
Proceeds from sale of building ($1,176,000 – 1,144,000 = 32,000) less accum. depr. ($399,000 + 121,000 – 517,000) = $3,000 accum. depr. for the sold building	29,000
Sale of machinery	50,000
Purchase of machinery ($918,750 – 125,000 – 1,188,000) = $394,250 less $166,000 = $228,250. $166,000 is a non-cash entry in exchange for shares ($199,500 – 60,000 – 305,500) = $166,000	(228,250)
Net cash flows from investing activities	(57,550)

Cash flows from financing activities:	
Issuance of preferred shares ($885,150 – $1,152,800)	267,650
Repurchase of common shares	(65,000)
Dividends paid ($326,550 – 5,000 common shares retirement – $58,700 net loss – $151,800) = $111,050 dividends for both preferred and common shares. Preferred shares dividend is $40,000. Common shares dividend is $71,050.	(111,050)
Net cash flows from financing activities	91,600

Net increase in cash	(15,500)
Cash, opening	21,000
Cash, closing	$ 5,500

Supplemental Disclosures:

Cash paid interest and income taxes are already reported as categories in operating activities when using the direct method. Only the non-cash items require supplementary disclosure (below).

Non-cash:

Machinery for $394,250 ($918,750 − $125,000 − $1,188,000) was purchased in exchange for $166,000 in common shares and $228,250 in cash.

Solution Notes:

* Bond amortization is a non-cash adjusting entry that affects interest expense in the income statement, therefore net income must be adjusted by $54,750 ($1,089,000 − $1,034,250) bond amounts, net of discount.

** Deferred tax is a non-cash transaction affecting income tax expense in the income statement, therefore net income must be adjusted by $42,900 ($69,300 − $26,400).

*** The change in investments held for trading is due to the unrealized loss included in the income statement. This has already been adjusted in step 3, so no further action is required. Memo item only.

b.

Bognar Ltd.
Statement of Cash Flows
For the year ended December 31, 2015

Cash flows from operating activities:	
Cash received from sales	$ 1,744,400
Cash paid for goods and services	(1,738,700)
Cash paid for interest	(71,750)
Cash received for income taxes	16,500
Net cash flows from operating activities	$ (49,550)

c. Indirect Method

Bognar Ltd.
Statement of Cash Flows (Indirect method)
For the year ending December 31, 2015

Cash flows from operating activities:	
Net loss	$ (58,700)
Non-cash items (adjusted from net income)	
Gain on sale of land	(24,200)
Depreciation ($121,000 + 82,500)	203,500
Loss on impairment of goodwill	66,000
Loss on sale of machine	10,800
Loss on Held for Trading investment	32,500***
Interest expense for bond payable	54,750*
Cash in (out) from operating working capital:	
Increase in accounts receivable	(108,000)
Increase in inventory	(146,000)
Decrease in accounts payable	(37,300)
Decrease in deferred taxes payable	(42,900)**
Net cash flows from operating activities	$(49,550)

* Bond amortization is a non-cash adjusting entry that affects interest expense in the income statement and is not included in the adjustments. Net income must, therefore, be adjusted by $54,750 ($1,089,000 − $1,034,250) bond amounts, net of discount.

** Deferred tax is a non-cash transaction affecting income tax expense in the income statement and is not included in the adjustments. Net income must, therefore, be adjusted by $42,900 ($69,300 − $26,400).

*** The change in investments held for trading asset account is due to the unrealized loss included in the income statement.

Supplemental Disclosures (Indirect Method):

Interest paid $71,750

($126,500 interest expense − bonds payable, net of discount of $54,750 ($1,034,250 − $1,089,000))

Non-cash:

Machinery for $394,250 ($918,750 − $125,000 − $1,188,000) was purchased in exchange for $166,000 in common shares and $228,250 in cash.

EXERCISE 20–7

a. Land – Entry #1

General Journal				
Date	Account/Explanation	PR	Debit	Credit
	Land (new)		100,000	
	Cash......................................			5,000
	Land (old)			80,000
	Gain on disposal of land			15,000

Land – Entry #2

General Journal				
Date	Account/Explanation	PR	Debit	Credit
	Land..		78,000	
	Cash......................................			78,000
	($98,000 − $100,000 + $80,000)			

Equipment – Entry #1

General Journal				
Date	Account/Explanation	PR	Debit	Credit
	Accumulated depreciation, equipment.......		15,000	
	Cash		2,000	
	Equipment...............................			15,000
	Gain on sale of equipment			2,000

Equipment – Entry #2

	General Journal			
Date	Account/Explanation	PR	Debit	Credit
	Accumulated depreciation, equipment.......		2,800	
	Loss on disposal of equipment..............		1,200	
	Equipment...............................			4,000

Equipment – Entry #3

	General Journal			
Date	Account/Explanation	PR	Debit	Credit
	Equipment.................................		9,000	
	Cash....................................			9,000
	($60,000 + $15,000 + $4,000 − $70,000)			

Equipment – Entry #4

	General Journal			
Date	Account/Explanation	PR	Debit	Credit
	Depreciation expense......................		4,400	
	Accumulated depreciation, equipment....			4,400
	($6,600 − $20,000 + $15,000 + $2,800)			

Lease – Entry #1

	General Journal			
Date	Account/Explanation	PR	Debit	Credit
	Equipment under lease		99,854	
	Obligations under lease..................			99,854
	PV = 20,000 PMT/AD, 8 I/Y, 6 N = $99,854			

Lease - Entry #2

	General Journal			
Date	Account/Explanation	PR	Debit	Credit
	Obligations under lease.....................		20,000	
	Cash....................................			20,000

Lease – Entry #3

	General Journal			
Date	Account/Explanation	PR	Debit	Credit
	Interest expense...........................		3,994	
	Interest payable.........................			3,994
	(($99,854 − $20,000) × 8% × 6 ÷ 12)			

Lease – Entry #4

General Journal				
Date	Account/Explanation	PR	Debit	Credit
	Depreciation expense........................		8,321	
	Accumulated depreciation, lease.........			8,321
	($99,854 ÷ 6 years × 6 ÷ 12)			

b.

Investing activities:
Payment on exchange of land   (5,000)
Purchase of land   (78,000)
Proceeds from sale of equipment   2,000
Purchase of equipment   (9,000)
Financing activities:
Payment on capital lease   (20,000)

c.

Partial statement of cash flows – indirect method
Cash flows from operating activities:
Net income   N/A
Non-cash items (adjusted from net income):
  Gain on disposal of land   (15,000)
  Gain on sale of equipment   2,000
  Loss on disposal of equipment   1,200
  Depreciation expense on equipment   4,400
  Depreciation expense on leased equipment   8,321
Cash in (out) from operating working capital:
  Increase in interest payable   3,994
Net cash flows from operating activities   N/A

Disclosures:

Interest paid ($3,994 interest expense – $3,994 increase in interest payable) $0

Non-cash items:

Land that originally cost $80,000 was exchanged for another tract of land with a fair value of $100,000 and a cash payment of $5,000.

Equipment worth $99,854 was acquired in exchange for a six year capital lease at an annual interest rate of 8%.

EXERCISE 20–8

Aegean Anchors Ltd.
Statement of Cash Flows (Indirect method)
For the year ended December 31, 2015

Cash flows from operating activities:

Net income	$ 288,000
Non-cash items (adjusted from net income)	
Depreciation	217,000
Equity in earnings of Vogeller	(26,400)
Loss on sale of equipment	3,000
Cash in (out) from operating working capital:	
Increase in accounts receivable	(95,640)
Decrease in inventory	(51,120)
Decrease in accounts payable	(73,200)
Decrease in income taxes payable	(10,800)
Net cash flows from operating activities	250,840
Cash flows from investing activities:	
Loan to Vancorp Ltd.	(350,000)
Cash payment received from Vancorp Ltd.	48,200
Sale of equipment	50,000
Net cash flows from investing activities	(251,800)
Cash flows from financing activities:	
Cash dividends paid	(102,000)
Net cash flows from financing activities	(102,000)
Net decrease in cash	(102,960)
Cash and cash equivalent, opening	(34,200)
Cash and cash equivalent, closing	$(137,160)

Disclosures:

Interest paid	$ 18,000
Interest received	11,300
Income taxes paid	181,000

Non-cash:

Aegean Anchors acquired equipment in exchange for a financing lease of $324,000. (Interest rate is 8%.)

Cash and cash equivalents:

	2015	2014
Cash	$ 33,960	$ 53,280
Bank overdraft	(171,120)	(87,480)
Total cash and cash equivalents	$(137,160)	$(34,200)

Chapter 21 Solutions

EXERCISE 21–1

Item	Type of Change
The useful life of a piece of equipment was revised from five years to six years.	AE
An accrued litigation liability was adjusted upwards once the lawsuit was concluded.	AE
An item was missed in the year-end inventory count.	E
The method used to depreciate a factory machine was changed from straight-line to declining balance as it was felt this better reflected the pattern of use.	AE
A company adopted the new IFRS for revenue recognition.	P
The accrued pension liability was adjusted downwards as the company's actuary had not included one employee group when estimating the remaining service life.	E
The allowance for doubtful accounts was adjusted upwards due to current economic conditions.	AE
The allowance for doubtful accounts was adjusted downwards because the previous estimate was based on an aged trial balance that classified some outstanding invoices into the wrong aging categories.	E
A company changed its inventory cost flow assumption from LIFO to FIFO, as the newly appointed auditors indicated that LIFO was not allowable under IFRS.	E
A company began to apply the revaluation model to certain property, plant, and equipment assets, as it was felt this presentation would be more useful to investors.	P

EXERCISE 21–2

a. Because the change in the useful life of the copyright is based on the existence of new information and new conditions, this would be a change in estimate and should be treated prospectively by adjusting amortization only for current and future years. The recording of the insurance premium is an accounting error as it should have originally been recorded as a prepaid expense. As such, this error should be accounted for retrospectively, correcting the error in the appropriate period and restating comparative information.

b. Original amortization = (100,000 − 10,000) ÷ 10 years = 9,000 per year

Amortization to 1 January 2016 = 9,000 × 3 years = 27,000

NBV at 1 January 2016 = (100,000 − 27,000) = 73,000

New rate = 73,000 ÷ 2 years = 36,500 per year

Note: Because the books are still open for 2016, we can correct the error for the current year as well as for the future year. However, the company would have to consider when the conditions changed that led to the estimate revision.

Journal entry:

General Journal				
Date	Account/Explanation	PR	Debit	Credit
	Amortization expense.......................		36,500	
	Copyright...............................			36,500

The insurance premium should have been reported as a prepaid asset when purchased, and recognized as an expense at $1,500 ÷ 12 = $125 per month. Thus, for the year ended December 31, 2015, only $125 × 2 = $250 should have been expensed. The following adjustment is required to correct this error:

General Journal				
Date	Account/Explanation	PR	Debit	Credit
	Insurance expense.........................		1,250	
	Retained earnings.......................			1,250

Note that this entry simply moves ten months of the insurance expense from 2015 to 2016. There is no need to adjust the prepaid as the insurance was fully utilized by the end of 2016. However, a comparative balance sheet, if presented, would need to include the prepaid expense of $1,250.

EXERCISE 21–3

In this case, there is both an accounting error and a change in accounting estimate. The error should be corrected first, retrospectively, and then the change in estimate can be applied.

Depreciation as originally calculated: $50,000 ÷ 5 years = $10,000 per year

Depreciation should have been: $50,000 − $5,000 ÷ 5 year = $9,000 per year

The following journal entry corrects the 2016 accounts:

General Journal				
Date	Account/Explanation	PR	Debit	Credit
	Accumulated depreciation....................		1,000	
	Retained earnings......................			1,000

The carrying amount is now $50,000 − $10,000 + $1,000 = $41,000

Double declining balance rate = (1 ÷ 5) × 2 = 40%

Therefore, 2017 depreciation will be $41,000 × 40% = $16,400

Note: Remember that residual values are not used in DDB calculations.

The following journal entry will record current year depreciation:

General Journal				
Date	Account/Explanation	PR	Debit	Credit
	Depreciation expense........................		16,400	
	Accumulated depreciation			16,400

EXERCISE 21–4

This is an accounting policy change that should be applied retrospectively. It means that the effect of the revaluations on prior years will need to be recorded, as well as the effects on depreciation expense. The changes are summarized below:

Year	Depr. Taken	Carrying Value	Revaluation	Revised Depr.	New CV
2013	25,000	725,000	800,000		800,000
2014	25,000	700,000	800,000	27,586	772,414
2015	25,000	675,000	800,000	27,586	744,828
2016	25,000	650,000	825,000	30,556	794,444

Note: On December 31, 2013, the building is revalued, creating a revaluation surplus of 75,000 (800,000 − 725,000). The revised depreciation is calculated as 800,000 ÷ 29 years = 27,586. This depreciation rate is used for 2014 and 2015. On December 31, 2015, the building is revalued creating a valuation surplus of 80,172 (825,000 − 744,828). The new depreciation rate to be used for 2016 and 2017 is 825,000 ÷ 27 years = 30,556.

On January 1, 2017, the total depreciation actually recorded is $100,000 (25,000 × 4). Total depreciation that would have been recorded under the revaluation model is $110,728 (25,000 + 27,586 + 27,586 + 30,556). The additional depreciation of 10,728 (110,728 − 100,000) needs to be adjusted to retained earnings. As well, the two revaluation surplus amounts 155,172 (80,172 + 75,000) need to be reflected in the revaluation surplus account.

The following journal entry adjusts the opening balances on January 1, 2017:

General Journal				
Date	Account/Explanation	PR	Debit	Credit
	Retained earnings		10,728	
	Building.		75,000	
	Accumulated depreciation.		69,444	
	Revaluation surplus (OCI)			155,172

Note: Remember that when using the revaluation model, previous accumulated depreciation amounts are eliminated when a revaluation occurs. Thus, the accumulated depreciation on December 31, 2016, would be $30,556, so the adjustment needs to be 69,444 (100,000 − 30,556). The building cost adjustment is based on the revised value (825,000) less the original cost recorded (750,000). This solution also assumes that there is no reclassification of OCI to retained earnings, as this is an optional treatment.

In 2017, the depreciation would be recorded as follows:

General Journal				
Date	Account/Explanation	PR	Debit	Credit
	Depreciation expense.		30,556	
	Accumulated depreciation			30,556

When the revaluation occurs on December 31, 2017, previous accumulated depreciation (the prior two years) is reversed and the revaluation is recorded:

General Journal				
Date	Account/Explanation	PR	Debit	Credit
	Accumulated depreciation.		61,112	
	Building			61,112

The carrying value of the building, prior to revaluation, is 763,888 (825,000 − 61,112).

The entry to record the revaluation on December 31, 2017, is:

General Journal				
Date	Account/Explanation	PR	Debit	Credit
	Revaluation surplus (OCI).		23,888	
	Building			23,888

This will reduce the carrying value of the building to $740,000.

EXERCISE 21–5

a. This is an accounting policy change that should be applied retrospectively. The following journal entry is required on January 1, 2016, to reflect the adjustment:

	General Journal			
Date	Account/Explanation	PR	Debit	Credit
	Inventory (opening)*........................		70,000	
	Retained earnings........................			49,000
	Income taxes payable....................			21,000

* The account used here will depend on whether the company uses a perpetual or periodic inventory system. With a periodic system, opening inventory is adjusted. With a perpetual system, cost of sales would be adjusted.

Note: Only the effect in 2015 needs to be considered. Inventory adjustments are self-correcting over a two-year period, so only the difference in the 2015 ending inventory needs to be adjusted.

b. The comparative column (2015) of the retained earnings statement would look like this:

	2015 (Restated)
Opening retained earnings as previously stated	$ 1,100,000
Accounting policy change, net of tax of $18,000	42,000
Opening balance, restated	1,142,000
Net income (restated)	282,000
Closing retained earnings	$ 1,424,000

The effect on opening retained earnings (i.e., January 1, 2015) reflects the inventory difference on December 31, 2014 (650,000 – 590,000) less tax. The net income for 2015 is calculated as follows:

Income as previously reported	$275,000
Reversal of 2014 difference, less tax	(42,000)
2015 difference, less tax	49,000
Revised net income	$282,000

EXERCISE 21–6

General Journal				
Date	Account/Explanation	PR	Debit	Credit
	Salaries payable............................		7,000	
	Salaries expense.........................			7,000
	Miscellaneous revenue......................		8,000	
	Accumulated depreciation...................		31,000	
	Vehicle..................................			40,000
	Depreciation expense...................			5,000
	Retained earnings..........................		6,000	
	Bad debt expense..........................		12,500	
	Allowance for doubtful accounts..........			12,500

AFDA s/b $1,500,000 × 2%   = $30,000

Current AFDA balance = $1,750,000 × 1%   = $17,500

Adjustment required $12,500

General Journal				
Date	Account/Explanation	PR	Debit	Credit
	Inventory....................................		12,000	
	Retained earnings..........................		8,000	
	Cost of sales............................			20,000

EXERCISE 21–7

Repair Expense Error

General Journal				
Date	Account/Explanation	PR	Debit	Credit
	Accumulated depreciation...................		2,250	
	Equipment...............................			9,000
	Depreciation expense....................			1,500
	Retained earnings..........................		8,250	

2016 depreciation recorded = $9,000 ÷ 6 years × 1 ÷ 2 = $750

2017 depreciation recorded = $9,000 ÷ 6 years = $1,500

Accrued Interest Omission

Accrued interest receivable on December 31, 2017 = $150,000 × 8% × 1 ÷ 12 = $1,000

Note: This represents the interest accrued between November 30 and December 31.

As the balance of the interest receivable account is $1,000, no adjustment is required as the balance is already correct.

Land Depreciation Error

Building depreciation as recorded:

$$2015: (1,000,000 - 50,000) \div 50 \times \tfrac{1}{2} = \quad \$\ 9,500$$

2016:	$19,000
2017:	$19,000
Total	$47,500

Building depreciation should be:

$$2015: (750,000 - 50,000) \div 50 \times \tfrac{1}{2} = \quad \$\ 7,000$$

2016:	$14,000
2017:	$14,000
Total	$35,000

	General Journal			
Date	Account/Explanation	PR	Debit	Credit
	Land..		250,000	
	Building			250,000
	Accumulated depreciation....................		12,500	
	Depreciation expense.....................			5,000
	Retained earnings			7,500

Note: Adjustment to accumulated depreciation is 12,500 (35,000 − 47,500), which is allocated to depreciation expense (14,000 − 19,000 = 5,000) for the current year, with the remainder allocated to retained earnings.

Machine Disposal Error

	General Journal			
Date	Account/Explanation	PR	Debit	Credit
	Accumulated depreciation....................		52,000	
	Factory machine.........................			50,500
	Gain on disposal........................			1,500

EXERCISE 21–8

Depreciation charges should be:

2015: 35,000 × 33.33% = 11,666

2016: (35,000 − 11,666) × 33.33% = 7,778

General Journal				
Date	Account/Explanation	PR	Debit	Credit
	Automobile		35,000	
	Accumulated depreciation			19,444
	Depreciation expense.......................		7,778	
	Income tax expense			1,556
	Retained earnings			18,667
	Income tax payable or deferred taxes			3,111

Retained earnings adjustment: (35,000 − 11,666) × 80%

Tax payable (deferred) adjustment: (35,000 − 19,444) × 20%

General Journal				
Date	Account/Explanation	PR	Debit	Credit
	Provision for lawsuit liability		750,000	
	Recovery of provision....................			750,000
	Deferred tax asset			150,000
	Deferred tax expense		150,000	
	Inventory		11,500	
	Sales		18,000	
	Cost of sales			11,500
	Accounts receivable			18,000
	Income tax payable		1,300	
	Income tax expense			1,300
	Retained earnings		48,000	
	Revenue.................................			60,000
	Income tax expense		12,000	

EXERCISE 21–9

	2016	2015
Reported net income	$1,200,000	$1,050,000
Adjustment for rent	60,000	(90,000)
Adjustment for office supplies	5,700	(4,500)
Adjustment for warranty	(6,000)	(38,000)
Adjustment for bonus	35,000	(12,000)
Corrected net income	$1,294,700	$ 905,500

Chapter 22 Solutions

EXERCISE 22–1

a. Sterling Inc. is owned by a close family member of a director of Kessel Ltd. This makes Kessel Ltd. and Sterling Inc. related parties. Disclosure is required for the relationship, any transactions during the period, and the fact that the amount was written off during the year.

b. Kessel Ltd.'s 35% share ownership of Saunders Ltd. would normally be presumed to give it significant influence, thus making the parties related. As such, the nature of the relationship and the transaction itself need to be disclosed. There is, however, no requirement to state that the transaction was at arm's length unless this fact can be verified.

c. Mr. Chiang is a member of the key management personnel of Kessel Ltd., making them related parties. Therefore, the details of the transaction need to be disclosed along with the nature of the relationship. As well, the guarantee of the mortgage should also be disclosed.

d. Even where there is economic dependence, regular supplier-customer relationships do not indicate related party relationships. Thus, no separate disclosure of this transaction is required.

EXERCISE 22–2

a. Without any further information about cross shareholdings, the presence of a single common director between companies does not, in and of itself, indicate a related party relationship.

b. A single investor has influence, but not control, over the other two companies. This would not normally indicate a related party relationship between the two associate companies.

c. Each of the directors is individually related to each of the companies. The presence of common directors does not, in and of itself, indicate a related party relationship between the two companies. However, IAS 24 does require an examination of the substance, and not just the form, of the relationships. If the five directors have demonstrated a pattern of acting together as a single voting unit, then it can be argued that as a group, they control the two companies. In this case, the presence of a common controlling group would indicate that the companies are related.

EXERCISE 22–3

a. January 8, 2018: The appropriation was approved after the year-end and there is no indication that this action was substantively enacted prior to the approval date. As such, this was not a condition present at year-end, and no adjustment is required. However, disclosure should be made, as this event will likely have a material effect on future operations.

b. January 27, 2018: Although the bonus was approved after year-end, it clearly relates to the financial results of the year and was committed under employment contracts that existed at the year-end. The bonus should thus be accrued on December 31.

c. February 3, 2018: The additional taxes should be accrued, as the tax dispute already existed at the year-end. The change will be treated prospectively, (i.e., adjust in 2017 only) unless it can be demonstrated that the previous provision was made in error.

d. February 21, 2018: This should be adjusted, as the error caused by the fraud existed at the reporting date. As well, because there is an illegal act involved, there may be further disclosures required.

e. March 16, 2018: Dividends should not be adjusted, as there is no obligation to pay them until they are declared. However, disclosure of the declaration should be made.

f. March 18, 2018: The condition did not exist at the reporting date, so no adjustment is required. If the loss of the machine will have a material effect on future operations, then disclosure should be made.

EXERCISE 22–4

Although the damage only appeared after the reporting period, the engineers have indicated that the problem may have been present for several years. This would indicate the presence of an adjusting event. However, a provision should not be made as there is no legal obligation to make the repairs at year-end, that is, the building could simply be abandoned rather than repaired. What should be done, however, is an impairment review under IAS 36, and any impairment of the asset should be recorded.

EXERCISE 22–5

The auditor needs to consider if there is sufficient evidence available to support a clean opinion, that is, that the financial statements have not been materially misstated. The correspondence with the legal counsel should be examined carefully in order to determine if the assertion that the outcome cannot be determined is supportable. Contingent liabilities are not accrued as provisions if there is only a possible, but not present, obligation that will only be settled by an uncertain future event, or if a present obligation cannot be reliably measured. If accrual of the provision is not warranted, disclosure in the notes is still required. In this case, the effects appear material, so the auditor will need to make sure that the appropriate note disclosures are made.

The auditor will also need to assess management's assertion that the plant will be closed if the legal case is lost as this may have a pervasive effect on future operations. The auditor may need to question the going concern assumption. Although it may be too early to make this determination, the compromise of the going concern assumption would lead to presentation of the financial statements using a different basis of accounting. If management refused to make this change, then the auditor would need to consider if a qualified, or adverse, opinion was warranted.

Even if the auditor is satisfied with the disclosures made, the pervasiveness of the matter may suggest the need for an emphasis of matter paragraph to be included in the audit report, thus drawing attention to the disclosures.

EXERCISE 22–6

Revenue test:

($289,000 × 10%) = $28,900. Business lines 1 and 4 meet this threshold.

Profit/(Loss) Test:

The total profits of $52,000 are greater than the total losses of $14,000, therefore ($52,000 × 10%) = $5,200

In absolute terms, ignoring the + and − signs, business lines 1, 2, and 4 meet this threshold.

Assets test:

($478,000 × 10%) = $47,800. Business lines 1 and 4 meet this threshold.

Conclusion:

Based on the tests above, business lines 1, 2, and 4 all meet at least one of the three tests above.

For the 75% or greater test ($289,000 × 75%) = $216,750

Sum of business lines 1, 2, and 4 (90,000 + 25,000 + 140,000) = $255,000

This test has been met by all of the reportable segments, which are business lines 1, 2, and 4. However, management can override all of these tests and report a business line as a reportable segment if they consider the segmented information to be useful to the stakeholders.

EXERCISE 22–7

Interim reporting has several challenges:

- Changes in accounting principles: If this change were to occur in the second or third quarter, how should this affect the first quarter interim financial statements? The general consensus is that, even if the change of a particular accounting policy, such as a depreciation method, is prospective, the annual change should be prorated to each of the interim accounting periods so as not to over/under state any specific quarter. This would lessen any tendency of management to manipulate accounting policies within a specific quarter in order to influence bonuses or operational results targets. Thus, even though the change in policy is applied prospectively for the fiscal year, if interim statements are prepared, the change in policy would be applied retroactively, but proportionally, between each quarterly period in order to smooth the results over each quarter for that fiscal year.

- Cyclical and seasonal swings experienced by businesses within a fiscal year: Revenue can be concentrated over a limited number of months, while expenses may be incurred on a monthly basis. If IFRS guidelines are followed, the principles of revenue recognition and matching (of expenses incurred to earn those revenues) will continue to be accrued and recorded within each of the interim periods and the same tests used for annual financial statements would be applied to the interim reports.

- Allocations for income taxes and earnings per share: The treatment requires each interim period to be independent of each other and for interim allocations to be determined by applying all the same tests as those used for the annual reports.

- Auditors: While some stakeholders continue to push for an examination of the interim reports in order to provide assurance, auditors are reluctant to express an opinion on interim financial statements. As such, there will always be a trade-off between the need for assurance through an audit opinion and the need to produce the interim report on a timely basis.

ASPE does not contain any guidance for reporting interim reporting or segmented information. The issues would be the same for companies following either IFRS or ASPE, except that IFRS requires more disclosures.

EXERCISE 22–8

a. Percentage (common-size) vertical analysis is as follows:

	2016	2015	2014
Net sales	100%	100%	100%
Cost of goods sold (COGS)	65%	60%	63%
Gross profit	35%	40%	37%
Selling and administrative expenses	20%	21%	22%
Income from continuing operations before income taxes	15%	19%	15%

The company's income before taxes declines in 2016 due to higher cost of goods sold (COGS) as a percentage of net sales, as compared with 2015. Moreover, the COGS in 2015 decreased by 3% from the previous year followed by a more than offsetting increase back to greater than the 2014 percentage levels. Was there a write-off of inventory in 2016 that would cause COGS to sharply increase from the previous year? More investigation would be needed to determine the reason for the difference. Selling and administration continues to slowly decrease over the three year period as a percentage of sales, suggesting that management may be taking steps to make operations more efficient. Separating the selling from the administration expenses would be a worthwhile drill-down into the numbers.

Horizontal (trend) analysis is as follows:

	2016	2015	2014
Net sales	119%	107%	100%
Cost of goods sold (COGS)	123%	102%	100%
Gross profit	113%	116%	100%
Selling and administrative expenses	109%	104%	100%
Income from continuing operations before income taxes	118%	132%	100%

This trend-line analysis highlights the jump in COGS between 2015 and 2016. Note how sales increased by 19% from 2014 while COGS increased by 23%. This divergent trend between these two accounts should be investigated further. Even though selling and administration expenses were shown to be dropping as a percentage of sales, these expenses actually increased over the two years. Further investigation of the increasing selling and administration costs might be necessary.

As can be seen from analysis of the two schedules above, different areas of operations may become targeted for further investigation depending on which schedule is examined. An area may not look particularly troublesome until another type of analyses is considered.

b. Limitations of these types of analyses include:

- Vertical/Common Size Analysis: The downside to this type of analysis is the need to avoid management bias, or the temptation to use various accounting policies in order to favourably change a gross margin for personal reasons such as bonuses or positive performance evaluations. For example, if a gross margin decreased from 40% to 35% over a two-year period, the decline could be a realistic reflection of operations, or it could be the result of a change in estimates or of accounting policy. For this reason, any change in the ratios should always be further investigated.

- Horizontal/Trend Analysis: If the company's operations are relatively stable each year, this analysis can be useful. However, changes in these ratios could also be due to a change in pricing policy and not due to actual transactions and economic events. Again, more investigation is necessary to determine if the increase is due to true economic events or changes in policy made by management.

It is important to remember that ratios are only as good as the data presented in the financial statements. For example, if quality of earnings is high, then ratio analysis can be useful, otherwise it may do more harm than good. Also, it is important to focus on a few key ratios for each category in order to avoid the risk of information overload; it is those few key ratios that should be investigated and tracked over time. It is also important to understand that industry benchmarks make no assurances about how a company compares to its competitors since the basis for the industry ratio may be different than the basis used for the company. As such, ratios provide good indicators for further investigation but they are not the end-point of an evaluation.

EXERCISE 22–9

a. Liquidity Ratio: Measures the enterprise's short-term ability to pay its maturing obligation:

Current ratio: $499,500 \div 393,200 = 1.27$

If a guideline of 2:1 is the norm for this industry, then this company's ratio is low. This company can meet its current debts provided that accounts receivable are collectible and inventory sellable. Too low could be an issue while too high could also be an issue and indicate an inefficient use of funds.

Quick ratio: $499,500 - 210,500 - 15,900 \div 393,200 = 0.69$

If a guideline of 1:1 is the norm for this industry then this company's ratio is low. More information is needed, such as historical trends or industry standards. Nearly 50% of the current assets are made up of inventory. Therefore, inventory risks such as obsolescence, theft, or competitors' products could affect this company.

b. Activity Ratio: Measures how effectively the enterprise is using its assets. Activity ratios also measure the liquidity of certain assets such as inventory and receivables (i.e., how fast the asset's value is realized by the company).

Receivables turnover: $550,000 \div 213,100 = 2.58$ times per year or every $365 \div 2.58 = 141$ days

If a guideline of 30 to 60 days is the norm for this industry, then receivables are being collected too slowly and too much cash is being tied up in receivables. Comparison to industry standards or historical trends would be useful.

Inventory Turnover: $385,000 \div 210,500 = 1.83$ times per year or every $365 \div 1.83 = 199$ days

An inventory turnover of less than three times per year appears to be very low. Too low may mean that too much cash is being tied up in inventory or there is too much obsolete inventory that cannot be sold. Too high can signal that inventory shortages may be resulting in lost sales. More information about the industry is needed.

Asset Turnover: $550,000 \div 1,369,500 = 0.40$

This ratio appears low. Too low means that this company uses its assets less efficiently to generate sales. Industry standards and historical trends would be useful.

EXERCISE 22–10

Liquidity:

$$\text{Current ratio} = \frac{\text{Current assets}}{\text{Current liabilities}} = \frac{1{,}296{,}500}{390{,}700} = 3.32 \text{ times}$$

Current ratio describes the company's ability to pay current liabilities as they come due.

This company's comparable current ratio is favourable.

Activity:

$$\begin{aligned}
\text{Days' sales in inventory} &= \frac{\text{Ending inventory}}{\text{COGS}} \times 365 \\
&= \frac{55{,}000}{500{,}000} \times 365 \\
&= 40 \text{ days}
\end{aligned}$$

Days' sales in inventory measures the liquidity of the company's inventory. This is the number of days that it takes for the inventory to be converted to cash. The company's days' sales in inventory are unfavourable when compared to the industry statistics.

$$\text{Total asset turnover} = \frac{\text{Net sales (or revenues)}}{\text{Average total assets}} = \frac{1{,}100{,}000}{1{,}977{,}500} = 0.56 \text{ times}$$

Total asset turnover describes the ability of a company to use its assets to generate sales—the higher the better.

This company's comparable asset turnover is unfavourable.

$$\begin{aligned}
\text{Accounts payable turnover} &= \frac{\text{COGS}}{\text{Average accounts payable}} \\
&= \frac{500{,}000}{265{,}200} \\
&= 1.89 \text{ times or every 194 days}
\end{aligned}$$

Accounts payable turnover describes how much time it takes for a company to meet its obligations to its suppliers. This company's accounts payable turnover is lower than the industry average which means they are preserving their cash longer by comparison.

Solvency/coverage:

$$\text{Debt ratio} = \frac{\text{Total liabilities}}{\text{Total assets}} = \frac{484{,}500}{1{,}977{,}500} = 24.50\%$$

Debt ratio measure how much of the assets are financed by debt versus equity. The greater the debt ratio, the greater the risk associated with making interest and principal payments. This company's comparable debt ratio is favourable.

Profitability:

$$\text{Profit margin} = \frac{\text{Net income}}{\text{Net sales (or revenues)}} = \frac{544{,}960}{1{,}100{,}000} = 49.54\%$$

Measures the company's ability to generate a profit from sales. This company's profit margin is favourable.

$$\text{Book value per common share} = \frac{\text{Equity applicable to common shares}}{\text{Number of common shares outstanding}}$$
$$= \frac{1{,}399{,}400}{15{,}900}$$
$$= \$88.01 \text{ per share}$$

When compared to its market price of $97, it appears that the market considers the earning power of its assets to be greater than the value of the company on its books. It follows that most profitable companies try to sustain a market value higher than the book value. Conversely, if the book value was higher than the market price, then the market considers that the company is worth less than the value on its books.

$$\text{Book value per preferred share} = \frac{\text{Equity applicable to preferred shares}}{\text{Number of preferred shares outstanding}}$$
$$= \frac{93{,}600}{3{,}744}$$
$$= \$25.00 \text{ per share}$$

There are no dividends in arrears, so this ratio reflects the average paid-in amount, or the call price if they are callable.

EXERCISE 22–11

a. i. Acid-test ratio for 2015:
$$\frac{75+310}{129+100} = 1.68{:}1$$
This is a liquidity ratio that is a more rigorous test of a company's ability to pay its short-term debts as they come due. Inventory and prepaid expenses are excluded from this ratio and only the most liquid assets are included.

   ii. The company's acid-test ratio is favourable relative to the industry average.

b. i. Accounts receivable turnover for 2015.
$$1,500 \div \frac{(310+180)}{2} = 6.12 \text{ times/year or every 59.64 days } (365 \div 6.12)$$

   ii. The company's accounts receivable turnover is unfavourable relative to the industry average because the company's turnover rate of 6.12 is lower than the industry rate of 8.2 times. In days, the company's rate is every 59.6 days (365 ÷ 6.12) as compared to industry's every 44.5 days (365 ÷ 8.2) which represents the average number of days to collect accounts receivable.

c. Using the return on assets ratio:

$$223 \div \frac{(2,189+1,050)^{*}}{2} \times 100 = 13.77\%$$

* (310 + 75 + 1,360 + 250 − 206 + 400) = 2,189;
(180 + 42 + 500 + 210 − 282 + 400) = 1,050

13.77% is higher (more favourable) than the industry average

EXERCISE 22–12

The balance sheet was strengthened from June 30, 2014 to June 30, 2015:

Debt financing (percentage of liabilities to total assets) decreased significantly, from 62.5% at June 30, 2014 ($75,000 ÷ $120,000)* × 100 to 5.91% at June 30, 2015 ($10,850 ÷ $183,550) × 100

* (1,800 + 7,000 + 950 + 1,100) = 10,850 total liabilities
(29,000 − 3,800 − 1,400 + 10,000 + 15,000 + 17,000 + 14,000 + 750 + 75,000 + 25,000 + 2,500 + 500) = 183,550 total assets

Equity financing (percentage of equity to total assets) increased from 37.5% at June 30, 2014 ($45,000 ÷ $120,000 × 100) to 94.09% at June 30, 2015 ($172,700 ÷ $183,550)* × 100

* (49,325 + 40,000 + 50,000 − 46,000 + 79,375 net income**) = 172,700
** Net income (2,000 + 314,000 − 22,000 − 20,000 − 123,900 − 4,875 − 5,000 − 1,200 − 17,900 − 41,750) = 79,375

EXERCISE 22–13

Calculations:

	2015	2014
Current ratio	(60 + 80 + 240) ÷ 180 = 2.11	(10 + 70 + 50) ÷ 75 = 1.73
Acid-test ratio	(60 + 80) ÷ 180 = 0.78	(10 + 70) ÷ 75 = 1.07

Yeo Company's current ratio improved significantly from 1.73 in 2014 to 2.11 in 2015. This means that in 2015, Yeo Company had $2.11 of current assets available to pay each $1.00 of short-term debt. However, the acid-test is a more strict measure of short-term debt-paying ability because it excludes less liquid current assets such as Yeo Company's merchandise inventory. Merchandise inventory is excluded because it is not available to pay short-term debt until it has been sold; there is also the risk that it might not be sold, due to obsolescence, spoilage, or poor sales. The acid-test for 2014 showed that there was $1.07 of quick current assets, or liquid current assets, available to pay each $1.00 of short-term obligations. The acid-test decreased in 2015 indicating that there was $0.78 of quick current assets available to pay each $1.00 of current liabilities, highlighting a potential cash flow problem. When there are insufficient current assets available to pay current liabilities, liquidity, or cash flow, is a concern, hence the relationship between short-term debt-paying ability and cash flow.

EXERCISE 22–14

Kevnar Corporation has strengthened its balance sheet because its debt ratio decreased from 2014 to 2015. Strengthening the balance sheet refers to how assets are financed— through debt or equity. The greater the equity financing, the stronger the balance sheet. This is because there is risk associated with debt financing (i.e., the risk of being unable to meet interest and/or principal payments). Therefore, although Kevnar Corporation has a greater percentage of its assets financed through debt than does Dilly Inc., it has increased equity financing which indicates a strengthening of the balance sheet because of the decrease in risk associated with debt financing.

Financing through equity also has its disadvantages. More equity-based financing can mean a dilution of ownership that results from the issuance of more shares to outside investors. More shareholders also means that there will be additional claims to the equity in the business. Conversely, debt does not dilute the ownership of a business since a creditor is only entitled to the repayment of the agreed-upon principal plus interest, so there is no direct claim on future profits of the business. Moreover, if the company is successful, the existing owners will reap a larger portion of the rewards than they would have if they had issued more shares to outside investors in order to finance the growth. Additionally, interest on debt can reduce net income and, hence, reduce income taxes, making equity financing potentially a more costly source of financing than debt. Because of the requirement to comply with federal laws and securities legislations, financing through issuance of shares is usually a more complicated and lengthy process than acquiring funds from debt sources. This certainly slows the financing process down but it can also add to the costs of equity based financing.

Made in the USA
Columbia, SC
27 April 2018